HOW TO BLOW HER
MIND IN BED

HOW TO BLOW HER MIND IN BED

The essential guide for any man who wants to satisfy his woman

siski green

sourcebooks casablanca

Published by Sourcebooks Casablanca, an imprint of Sourcebooks, Inc.
P.O. Box 4410, Naperville, Illinois 60567–4410
(630) 961–3900
Fax: (630) 961–2168
www.sourcebooks.com
First published in 2007 by Piatkus Books Ltd, London.

Library of Congress Cataloging-in-Publication Data

Green, Siski.
  How to blow her mind in bed : the essential guide for any man who wants to satisfy his woman / Siski Green.
     p. cm.
  Includes bibliographical references and index.
  1. Sex instruction. I. Title.
  HQ56.G68 2008
  613.9'6082—dc22

                          2008032076

          Printed and bound in the United States of America
                        RRD 10 9 8

To Josecito, te amo más!

Contents

Your Silent Signals
Her Silent Come-Ons
The Approach
Real Girls Tell All

Why You Must Kiss
Kissing Technique
Timing and Locations
Real Girls Tell All

Acknowledgments

Thank you to my wonderful family for being supportive without being nosy; Graeme Gourlay, an inspirational editor and publisher, for giving me my first career break and giving me the confidence to keep moving forward; to Morgan Rees for encouraging me to write about sex and relationships and to always strive for perfection; to Jake at Conville and Walsh for his perseverance and support.

I learned a lot by reading some other fantastic sex books: Lou Paget's *The Big O: How to Have Them, Give Them, and Keep Them Coming*, Dr Sadie Allison's *Tickle Your Fancy: A Woman's Guide to Sexual Self-Pleasure*, Tracey Cox's *Superhotsex*, and Nancy Friday's *My Secret Garden*. I've also had some great advice from sex counselor Dr Pam Spurr, psychosexual therapist Vicki Ford, and Relate counselor Paula Hall.

I'd also like to say thank you to Joe Mackie, Rob Kemp, Hecks, Nicky, Pip, Ray, Jo and Justin, Elain, Kirsten, Blommers, and anyone else I may have momentarily forgotten—for talking, listening, and just being there.

Please see www.siskigreen.com for more about me and to email any tips and techniques you'd like to share.

Introduction

I view sex as I do eating: it's an essential part of my life, but I try hard not to take it for granted. And, like eating, I like to think about sex even when I'm not doing it. Just as I would consider the ingredients I'm going to cook with, which spices to add, and how I'll heat it up and serve it, I've spent a lot of time thinking about the different ways people can explore sex. What makes my thoughts about sex different, though, is that I get paid to put them on paper—something I can't claim for my enthusiastic home cooking.

Since I started writing about sex five years ago, I've had everyone from the plumber to family members telling me their sexual secrets and concerns. Sex, it seems, is something we've all got lots to say about, only we tend not to say it out loud. That's a shame because, like great recipes handed down from generation to generation, I think there are probably a lot of fantastic sexual tricks and techniques that we could all learn from (and if you'd like to share them, please feel free to email them anonymously to the address given on page xii).

So, based on what I've learned through my own experiences as well as hundreds of ideas and techniques I've learned from others, I've tried to provide an insight into what sex is like for a woman to give you an idea of what feels great, what she hates, and the things she wishes you'd do more of. I want you to finish this book feeling that you've got a better understanding of women, that you've learned exactly how to make her feel fantastic in bed, and, most importantly, that you're so charged up with new ideas that you just can't wait to try them out.

Remember, though, that in sex, just like in cooking, each chef has his or her own favorite ingredients, preferred techniques, and signature dish. This book, like a recipe book, is here to guide and advise you—but if you'd like to add a little more salt or a little less pepper, keep things boiling a little longer, or skip a particular recipe completely, please do so. There is only one absolute rule when it comes to phenomenal sex: there *are* no rules, just good advice. And that's what I hope to provide in this book.

Flirting

Here's a fact that may surprise you: every day you pass at least one beautiful woman who would consider getting naked with you. Open your eyes a little wider and you might just see her. And experts say that most women—beautiful or otherwise—decide whether they'd like to get naked with you between 90 seconds and four minutes of meeting you. Yet, despite an ever-wider variety of ways to meet other singles—from matchmaking to Internet dating—there are now more single men and women than ever before. So what's going on?

Well, to begin with, you give off the wrong signals a lot of the time. And even when you've got that right, you lack the ability to read her subtle signals. Men are notoriously inept at reading non verbal cues from women, and in today's fast-paced society this ineptitude results in hundreds, if not thousands, of missed opportunities. In one study undertaken by the BBC, men were twice as likely to categorize facial expressions incorrectly when compared with women. And yet, when scientists assessed what women were checking out when they met a man, 55 percent of their first impression was based on body language, 38 percent on the tone and speed of your voice, and a paltry 7 percent on what you're actually saying! All the more reason to discover the surprisingly obvious ways women show their attraction to you and use it to your full advantage.

Your Silent Signals

See it as your shortest interview ever: you've got a few minutes to convince a woman you want the job and that she should consider you for the role of lover. Find out what she's thinking about your body, what you're wearing, and your posture.

Work your body

Believe it or not, a woman will try to size up what's in your underpants in the same way that you check out a woman's breasts or behind when you see her for the first time. To assess this, researchers making a program about sexual attraction filmed people walking down the street. As a woman passed a man, she would look at his face, then down between his legs, just as a man looked toward a woman's breasts and then her hips. Most women had no idea they did this.

What is she looking for? A reasonable-sized package of course! Size does matter; if it didn't, humans wouldn't have evolved to have larger penises than their ape relatives. Our cousins the chimps have penises half the size of a human's, and the poor gorilla has an average length of just 4cm (1½ in). This would indicate that in prehistoric times human females had a preference for longer and bigger penises, and over time, the average penis size grew to be approximately 15cm (6in). So to make sure she knows you're adequate in the trouser department—get a proper-fitting pair of jeans and give all the girls something to look at.

What if there's not much to show?

If you're a fan of baggies or you're not convinced your package is big enough, don't worry—there are plenty of other ways you can use your body to attract a woman. The way you stand, for example, will tell her what you'll be like in bed. One foot behind the other says you're a bit shy or nervous; a wide leg stance says you're feeling confrontational; and standing with your feet hip-width apart, facing toward her, says you're just right.

Your back and chest give out even more messages: a stiff, upright posture will make you look like you'll be unloving and quite possibly uptight; sticking your chest out too far will make you look as though you'll try to dominate; rounded shoulders make you look lacking in confidence; and letting your stomach hang out makes you look like you just don't give a s*it.

Take a deep breath then exhale, and your shoulders will naturally drop back and down and your chest will fill out; lift your chin a little so that you look confident and open; and only ever put one hand in a pocket—two makes you look like you're playing with something in there.

And to give her even more to look at up top, rather than down below, keep your hair in great condition. Subconsciously, both men and women are attracted to mates with strong hair, because if it shines, is vibrant in color, and is free of dandruff, it gives the impression you're getting essential nutrients in your diet. A clean, fresh-smelling head of hair will also encourage her to nuzzle your ear or neck…and no woman will want greasy, dirty hair on her bedroom pillows. But don't be put off if you haven't got much of your own hair—a closely shaved head is equally sexy. Touching your shaved head as you talk to a woman is a sexy move. The scalp is an incredibly erotic part of the body—just ask any woman who gets a regular head massage at the hairdresser. Moving your open hand over it, from the nape of the neck upwards, is damned sexy, because it draws her attention to an erotic part of your body, your neck.

Let her know she's sexy

So you've clocked a woman you'd like to get to know better, and you want to show her you're interested, so you smile. Great move—just make sure you give it your all. That first smile is like the kick off at a football game: it sets the tone for the rest of the game. For a fighting chance, you need to put some effort into it; a half-hearted, close-mouthed smile just won't cut it. Instead, make sure your message is clear—when you crack a genuine smile, you show your teeth and all your facial muscles are involved. Social anthropologist Helen Fisher has studied sexual attraction in different cultures around the world, and the teeth-flashing smile, along with raised eyebrows, is a universally recognized signal of sexual interest.

If a big toothy grin isn't something you can bring yourself to attempt, do the classic double take. Aside from a smile, the double take is the single most effective nonverbal move you can master. Catch her eye, look away, then look back within just a few seconds, and it's like saying, "I can't believe how sexy you are" out loud. But make sure you hold her gaze for just a few seconds longer than would normally be considered polite on the second look, and now flash her that warm smile.

Doing this is a real ego boost for the woman in question, and costs you nothing at all. If she doesn't respond, you just go back to whatever you were doing—drinking your beer, walking down the street, shopping for milk—but if she does react positively, your pathway is clear for approach, which we'll get to later.

Move closer

If the woman you've set your sights on is a colleague or a friend of a friend, there are other nonverbal ways you can increase your potential attraction. To begin with, get your handshake right. Firmness is a good start; by far the worst handshake is one where your hand is limp and clammy. But how you look after your hands is also important—she knows that if she goes to bed with you, those hands are going to be all over her.

And even if she doesn't touch your hands, she will notice your fingernails. If you chew them, if they're dirty, if they're too long—whatever is wrong with them, she'll pick up on it and will be less attracted to you. This is largely due to a subconscious assessment of your hygiene: your fingers will be touching her in places where germs and bacteria are easily transferred.

Where you put your hands is also a great way to get her gaze to land where you want: if you've got great biceps, let your hand move over your nut-crackers; if you've got a washboard stomach, give it a little pat or gentle rub; and touching the back of your neck is always a winner. Lifting your arm to touch the back of your neck with your hand does two things: it gives her a better chance of catching your personal scent and it reveals a sensitive part of your body, your wrists.

Showing your inner wrist is the equivalent of her revealing her neck, an erotic body part. It's a vulnerable, sensitive part of your body because the blood is so close to the surface. But solid wrists are also a sign of strength. It's one of the physical aspects of a man that makes him different from a woman, and so in the same way that you find tiny ankles or a slim neck sexy, she finds thick wrists attractive.

You smell good!

Each of us has a genetic "odor"—and if she leans in close or you raise your arm (to touch the back of your head, as mentioned earlier), you're unwittingly letting her get a good sniff. In an Austrian study, women were given T-shirts that had been worn by a number of men. The women were shown photographs of the T-shirts' owners and were asked to smell each T-shirt while simultaneously looking at the owner's photo. This was repeated a number of times, but the women were given a different combination of T-shirts and photos each time. When the women were asked which T-shirt-photo combination they preferred, each woman picked the same T-shirt that she had picked previously, regardless of which photograph she had been shown. The scent on the T-shirts caused the women to see a man as more attractive, regardless of what he actually looked like.

Attraction to a particular male scent is peculiar to the individual woman. This "scent code" prevents us mating with people we're closely related to, and helps us choose mates who will give the best chance of healthy offspring.

Giving off "stay away" signals

Sometimes you inadvertently give out the message that you'd rather not meet a woman—this is never more so than when you're with a big group of mates. If you're the kind of guy who goes out regularly with his mates and never has any luck with the ladies, it could be because you look like you're having too much fun. Men in a big group, particularly when they're laughing loud and hard, are unlikely to find much success (and by "success" I don't mean mauling a drunken girl; I'm referring to attracting women who are still sober enough to make a conscious decision).

All that standing around and making banter with your male buddies can further hinder your chances with the ladies. Studies have shown that men in groups are more competitive and display competitive behavior; this helps to raise testosterone levels, which makes you more aggressive and louder. While these traits might help give you raised status among your male friends, they're likely to scare potential girlfriends off.

To look approachable, hang out with no more than two other friends, and if you see someone who catches your eye, stand slightly apart from the others, and indicate your interest with the all-important smile and double take. If you shake off some mates, you'll get far more dates.

Wearing it well

You have a few more tricks up your sleeve—but make sure that sleeve is cashmere. A woman's love of cashmere and silk isn't about material wealth; it's about enjoying how those materials feel. For example, cashmere feels particularly soft because it has finer hairs than sheep's wool (the very softest is gathered from the Cashmere goat's underbelly). Think about how your clothes feel as well as look, and you'll find women getting a lot more hands-on with you.

How your clothes fit is really important, too. When female readers of several women's magazines were asked to say how they'd improve men's looks, 44 percent said they'd prefer them to wear snug sweaters rather than shapeless and baggy ones; 55 percent said your jeans are too loose; and 37 percent said your suit needs to be tailored properly. She doesn't want you to look like you spend hours in front of the mirror—she just wants to see that manly body under all those layers. Use a tape measure around your chest to find what size you should be wearing, and ask for a proper fitting when you next go clothes shopping. Better still, ask a female friend to come with you to advise.

And one final word of warning: be extremely wary of leather clothing. Like fast, red sports cars, leather jackets usually contain unattractive men trying to look good/young/rich. Lose it. If you're overweight, a leather jacket will serve only to draw attention to your size. If you're slim, a leather jacket can make you look pigeon-chested.

Make sure your jacket fits properly on your shoulders; one that hangs over the edges of your shoulders makes them look rounded and your posture bad. Instead, draw attention to your slimness with a fitted style.

The shoes, the shoes

If you've put all this effort into your clothing, don't forget your shoes. It is a cliché, but for good reason, that women do judge you by what's on your feet. Caring about how the shoes work with the rest of your outfit, and keeping them clean and relatively new-looking, shows that you pay attention to detail.

That's attractive in a man. A man who cares enough to keep his shoes shining, and ensures they match his trousers and socks, will also care enough to know that she likes freesias rather than roses, a cappuccino rather than a latte, or a kiss on the forehead before she goes to sleep.

Her Silent Come-Ons

Now for those non verbal cues she's giving you, the ones you're usually oblivious to. Spend some time watching other men and women interact with each other and you'll observe most of these signs.

She's looking hot!

So she's made an effort to look good—had her hair done and bought a new dress—and your tongue is scraping the floor as you watch her walk through the room. But, the sad truth is that you're actually less likely to succeed when she's looking her finest.

She may have gone to the hair salon with the intention of looking her best, and it may even be that she's done it with the intention of catching a man's eye. It may even be your eye she wants to catch. It's unfortunate, but drawing lots of attention to herself in this way will mean she'll be getting lots of people—men and women—talking to her, taking up her time, and distracting her from you, or any other man for that matter.

Don't get disheartened, however, because there are certain days when single women are more likely to find you attractive. Studies have shown that when women are at their most fertile—14 days before the first day of their period—they are also at their most easily aroused. And a study undertaken in Austria assessed how much clothing women were wearing when going out to a nightclub at different times of the month. They were found to wear far more revealing clothing at their most fertile time of the month. (The same change was not observed in women on the contraceptive pill, however.)

Who turned the heat up?
Body heat has more to tell you about how she's feeling. If she's attracted to you, and you're talking, her attraction could cause her to shed some layers of clothing. When she feels sexual attraction, blood rushes to her cheeks, her lips, and her genitals, and her body temperature rises a little, making her look and feel flushed.

Most of these physiological symptoms are emulated by her through the use of make-up—women spend vast sums on blush and lipstick in order to look more beautiful, but few realize that they're simply mimicking a natural state of sexual arousal.

And if you experience "butterflies" in your stomach when you look at her or touch her, you're also feeling a physiological response to sexual arousal. As blood rushes to your genitals in anticipation of sex, it drains from the stomach, creating that funny feeling in your stomach.

Recognizing the look of lust

Despite what most erotic magazines and films might lead you to believe, a non-smiling, smoldering look isn't the best indicator that she wants to get naked with you. She's far more likely to giggle like an idiot when she's attracted to you. Studies of women and their interactions with men have revealed that flirtation has the same pattern in any culture—she lowers her chin, raises her eyes, and covers her face as she laughs. You didn't really think your one-liners were funny, did you?

Once you're talking, check out her eyes—is she blinking a lot? It's not because she's got something in her eye, it's because she likes you. Batting her eyelids, fluttering her eyelashes, making eyes at you—whatever you want to call it, blinking is a sure sign of attraction. Studies have revealed that women blink more times per minute when they find a man sexy.

Keep looking at her eyes for more clues: where she moves them when looking at your face is a good indicator of attraction, too. We all look at people's mouths when we talk, but with someone we're attracted to, we do it more often. If her eyes move from yours down to your mouth, back up and back down again rather than just occasionally wandering to your mouth, then you could be in for a good night. Be aware, though, if you're in a loud venue, she may just be lip-reading!

The Approach

Now you know how to catch her eye, find the right place and the best way to make your approach.

Find your place

Bars and pubs are full of partner-hungry people—you can almost smell the desperation in the air. Instead, approach women in places they don't expect it. Here are some places to try:

Department stores/unisex clothes shops

Shops are a virtually untapped date resource. The only men seen there are usually sitting outside the changing rooms looking miserable, and yet meeting a woman is easier here than in a bar or pub.

The trick: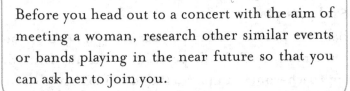

Ask her advice and explain that you're buying something for your sister or another female relative. This lets her know you're single, otherwise you'd have asked your girlfriend/wife for advice, and it gives you an opportunity to engage her in conversation.

Music concerts

Having a common interest gives you an opportunity to talk to each other, plus it gives you a great excuse to ask her on a second date—to another concert.

The trick:

Before you head out to a concert with the aim of meeting a woman, research other similar events or bands playing in the near future so that you can ask her to join you.

Salsa class

A higher ratio of women to men attend dancing classes and the sexy, close style of salsa is a great way to break down barriers and get comfortable with strangers.

The trick:

Learn some of the moves at a small salsa class, then move to a bigger group. Showing her you've got some level of skill will impress her and make you look smoother on the dance floor.

Walking the dog

Men who care about animals are seen as being more caring overall—something women look out for.

The trick:

Ask her about her dog. Or, if she doesn't have one, tell her about yours. Don't do this if you're in a secluded spot—approaching a woman in a place like that is just plain scary.

Getting your approach style right

Women love the cheeky guy best. Of course, there are exceptions—some women prefer the strong, silent type, or the deep thinker, or even arrogant know-it-alls—but cheeky guys get the best overall results.

Teasing is a form of affection in many cultures. It's a way to get people relaxed and laughing, but it is also a form of flirtation. Like play fighting at school, it's a way of encouraging interaction, and if you can achieve getting someone of the opposite sex riled, it's often a good indicator that they like you. Women tend not to get so irritated with people they don't care about at all.

Where to draw the line

Not sure how to differentiate between cheeky and plain rude? Use this brief guide:

Cheeky	Tickling her.
Plain rude	Pinching her bottom.
Cheeky	Laughing when she says something silly.
Plain rude	Laughing when she trips or spills a drink.
Cheeky	Coyly asking her to feed you a mouthful of what she's eating.

Plain rude	Grabbing a chip off her plate.
Cheeky	Saying, "You're quiet now, but I bet that when you let loose, you really go wild."
Plain rude	Saying, "You're quiet now, but I bet you're a screamer in bed."

Getting your "sell" right

When you're talking about your life, make everything positive for at least the first five dates. That doesn't mean you have to say your life is fantastic when it's not, but you must avoid telling her about your problems at work, difficulties with your family or bad feelings about the world in general. That can all come later. Women are naturally inclined to listen, and she may even seem to be encouraging you to talk through any problems, but telling her your negative thoughts at such an early stage won't make her want to get you naked. Worse, rather than having had a fun night filled with laughter, she'll leave the date feeling like she's helped you through your problems—that's nice but not sexy.

And while you're there, aim to show her that you do interesting things with your spare time—mention your drumming class or your love of Tai Bo, for example, and she's likely to find you more attractive. Women are naturally attracted to men who display varying abilities and adaptability. She may not have any personal interest in your hobby or pastime, but the fact that you've got one shows you're not a one-dimensional guy.

Don't talk about any one part of your life for more than a few minutes at a time—it will give that aspect too big an emphasis. A man who has spent too long a time focusing on one particular aspect of his life, be it his body, his career, or eating, comes across as obsessive and single-minded—not great traits for a healthy relationship. A balanced individual who takes care and interest in all these areas is far more attractive.

Time to ask her out!

You've been talking, the pub's about to close, the café owner is giving you dagger looks, or the museum security guard is ushering you toward the exit—now is the time to do your asking. Do it!

I'll admit it, not every woman you meet would like to lock lips with you, but the biggest complaint from single women is that men simply don't ask, so take the chance whenever you can. During an informal experiment undertaken for use in a television program, male participants were told to go up to complete strangers and ask these women if they would sleep with them that night. They didn't ask for a date, or for a chat—they asked straight out if the woman would sleep with them. One out of ten said yes—without any chatting up or preamble. Just imagine what would happen if you asked ten women out. Take any opportunity you can.

When you ask her out, be careful about what you suggest. If she was a total stranger before tonight, chances are an offer of dinner might be too full on. Unless she knows you, it's difficult to say yes to a drink, let alone a dinner date, even if she thinks you're sexy as hell—after all, you could be a psycho. So, to forestall any concerns she might have, ask her to bring a friend or offer to meet her somewhere she'll feel safe.

Do some research: find out what concerts, gigs, club nights are on, and so on, then use this in your approach. Explain that you're going and why it'll be good, then suggest she and a friend come along. Not only is this a more casual way to ask a woman out; it also means that she can bring a friend, so she'll feel safe in the knowledge that she can get to know you with her friend as backup if she wants to leave.

Bring a friend along, too. Meeting up in a group situation takes the pressure off both of you. Conversation is easier to keep flowing and she's more likely to be confident and relaxed in the company of a friend—and who knows, maybe your friend and hers will get it together as well. Double dating really does have its advantages.

Real Girls Tell All

SERENA explains why she fell for her current boyfriend:

"I was wearing a boldly patterned flowery dress and having a good time in the pub with my friends, when John passed me on his way to the bar. He stopped, flashed me a big smile, and said, "Only a sexy princess like you could carry off my grandma's curtains," and pointed to my dress. I was insulted, of course, but I was also flattered. I laughed, but I kind of wanted to get back at him, too. Luckily, when he was coming back from the bar, someone accidentally nudged him and he spilt beer down the front of his trousers. It did look like he'd had an accident in the toilet. I laughed and said, "Was it time to go?" I thought he'd be annoyed, or at least embarrassed, but he just flashed me another one of those smiles, winked, and said, "Time to go? I'm ready whenever you are...just let me get my coat." Then we started chatting and he kept making me laugh, teasing me and being silly. By the end of the night, all I wanted to do was get him out of there so I could give him a big kiss. Which is exactly what I did!"

WENDY on the best one-night stand she's ever had:

"The minute I saw him I knew I wanted to get naked with him. He was average looking, but he gave me a beaming smile across the bar—his eyes really lit up as though he'd seen something amazing. He had great shoulders, I could see that through the casual sports jersey he was wearing, and he had fantastic hands—good, strong fingers but with smooth skin. I could easily imagine them on my body. We made love all night. I say "made love," although clearly we weren't in love, as we hardly knew each other, but it felt like very warm, affectionate, passionate sex. Not like you'd expect a one-night stand to be. There was lots of kissing, and exploring each other's bodies—I did things I hadn't before, like touching myself while I was on top so he could see—it was just brilliant.

"We had hardly spoken to each other during the night, it had all been sex and sleep, and somehow we both knew it was just a one-night thing. In the morning we had sex one more time and I left. Kissing good-bye, we both grinned at each other. Never underestimate the power of a smile!"

KIRSTY describes how she met her husband:

"I'd been Internet dating for quite a while before I met my husband. He was really friendly and told me he really liked my shoes. I'd only bought them that day, so I was pleased and also impressed that he'd noticed. Talking to him was easy, and I found myself using excuses to keep touching his arm. By the end of the night I knew I definitely wanted to see him again. We kissed as we said good-bye and I saw him again a few days later. We've been married for a year and a half now."

2

Kissing

Kissing is a language all of its own—it has grammar and punctuation, and some people are better at using it to their advantage than others. In kissing, just like language, your "sentences" should never be so long that you run out of breath. You have "punctuation" in the form of breathing stops, like commas, and exclamation marks if the kiss goes particularly well. Just like using words to express yourself, kissing can say a thousand things, too: hello, good-bye, I love you, I want you, and so on. And the way you kiss not only sends out a signal about the message you're trying to convey, it also tells a potential mate whether or not she wants to take it any further. Kissing is your key to convincing any woman to get into bed with you, to love you, and to choose you as her partner.

Why You Must Kiss

The moment your lips meet hers, several decisions are made: will she go to your place? Will she see you again? Will she fall in love with you? To understand why, read on.

Chemical reactions

People really can go weak at the knees with a kiss—the chemical reaction in your body is intense, and it's all because your body is preparing for sex. A simple kiss not only requires 20 muscles to coordinate but also the process sets off a chain of other reactions in your body: the hypothalamus in your brain activates neurons; the pituitary gland secretes hormones to target the ovaries and testes; and a release of dopamine, endorphins, and phenyl ethylamine is triggered, and attaches to pleasure receptors in the brain, giving you a feeling of giddy euphoria. Chemical cues are sent through the spinal cord, and then the adrenal glands begin to produce and secrete nor epinephrine and epinephrine (otherwise known as adrenalin). This in turn increases your heart rate and hastens the breakdown of glycogen in your muscles and liver, to help provide you with energy for the sex to come.

How do you know she likes you?

The girl can't help it. Looking at someone's mouth when you're attracted to them is instinctive, and most people do it without even realizing it. Although we also look at friends' mouths when they talk, we do it less frequently, preferring to look them in the eyes. Count how many times she does it in between looking at your eyes—people who are attracted to each other tend to move in a near-constant triangle from eye to eye to mouth and round again.

The handy thing about this is that when you lean in to kiss her, she's prepared because she's focused on your lips anyway. Watch two people kiss and see how their eyes wander to each other's lips just beforehand. If her eyes are locked on your lips, your runway is clear for approach. Just make sure it's a soft landing…(see "Kissing Technique," pages 31-40, for kissing skills).

Kissing someone new

When you kiss someone new, your body releases dopamine and norepinephrine, two natural stimulants that give you that feel-good rush. Over months, as you get used to kissing each other, your body doesn't release the same amount and so it doesn't feel quite so exciting anymore—the result is that you both tend not to kiss for as long as you used to or as often. But, by making the effort to kiss, you're still creating a whirl of activity in your body. Kissing stimulates the brain. There are a huge number of receptors devoted to picking up sensations from the lips—these helped our ancestors discern whether food was poisonous or not. And it's this extra-sensitivity that makes kissing feel so great.

Bad kisses

A bad kiss pulls the curtains on a relationship faster than anything about your appearance or that you can say. But a bad kiss doesn't necessarily mean bad technique. Of course, if you smash your face into hers, grind your teeth against her lips, and slobber down her chin, she may be wondering how long it'll take to teach you how to do it properly, but even so, she may find your kiss is the one she's looking for. Why? It's all down to chemicals. Women can smell whether they find you attractive or not. (See You Smell Good!" on page 8). This effect is due to her subconscious desire to mate with a suitable male—to increase her potential offspring's survival, a woman needs to choose a man with very different disease-fighting abilities from her own. And that's the information she gains from your odor. If it's different enough from hers, she'll find you attractive. This also explains why, despite millions of dollars being spent on aftershave and cologne each year, 58 percent of women would rather you didn't smell of anything at all (according to a survey undertaken by four women's magazines).

So what can you do about it? Not much. But you can ease your worries if a woman doesn't return your calls after the first kiss by telling yourself that she didn't have the right genes for you anyway.

Kissing keeps you a couple

There's a direct correlation between how much time you spend kissing and satisfaction in the relationship. In fact, psychologists can predict a break up on the basis of lack of kissing and cuddling, in a marriage.

One reason kissing is so intimate is because it doesn't involve the genitals, and therefore you're not doing it for selfish reasons—that is, to give yourself an orgasm. But it's also because being face-to-face with your partner makes it a loving act that's difficult to fake. If you don't kiss her, or you only kiss her before you want sex, that genuine intimacy is lost. You don't have to stick your tongue in her mouth every time you see her to maintain that closeness. In fact, the inside of her mouth has fewer nerve endings than the red-colored part outside. Kissing her on the lips with your mouth closed can be very sensuous if you let your mouth linger on hers, pull away, and kiss her again. Do it when she least expects it—when you're out shopping or in the car, for example—and it's guaranteed to make her really smile.

While sex without kissing can and does happen—hey, it might even be great—you're missing a trick by omitting it. Lip language is key to arousal and gives her a good sense of how you feel about her while you're having sex. And kissing hello and good-bye are, like I said earlier, the punctuation marks of your loving language. Making the effort to kiss when you say hello—pausing, looking into her eyes, putting your hands around her face, and gently pressing your lips to hers—tells her you've been thinking about her, you've missed her, and you want to show her how you feel. A look from your partner can trigger memories and fantasies within the brain. Signals from the visual parts of the brain are transmitted to the hypothalamus, where they influence the start of sexual behavior. You can't buy that effect with any gift, no matter how big—it's all in your eyes.

A kiss can speak a thousand words

Kissing is great for so many reasons: it's not just for sex; often it can say "Sorry" more effectively than a thousand words. But to work it's got to be genuine, and if you're saying "Sorry," tongues are banned. This is an intimate, loving kiss, where you look into her eyes to let her know she can trust you, where your lips are soft on hers so she knows you're sorry, and where your hands are around her face so she gets the message that you're being serious. By kissing you'll help release some feel-good chemicals in her brain and yours, helping you both to overcome your mood.

Note: Never, ever kiss her during an argument if she's talking. In your mind it might be a romantic way of saying, "I love you and I'm sorry, so please stop having a go at me." In a woman's mind, it's the equivalent of saying, "Shut up, you silly bitch." Steer clear.

Kissing Technique

A woman will dismiss a potential lover based solely on her enjoyment of the first time your lips meet—and she will also make the decision to go home with you based on it. There's no single "magic" technique that works for all women, but there are a few guidelines that will help.

Moving in

She snuggles in, so you both know she's interested, but then her head is stuck to your shoulder making that lips-meet-lips position difficult to engineer. In an ideal world, she raises her head toward you after you've just said something charming...you lean in and you kiss. In the real world, she's far more likely to remain glued to your shoulder all the way home, leading to a fumbling, embarrassing attempt at a good-bye kiss.

The trick is to use your hands, or the hand furthest from her, more specifically. All you need to do is move it to the side of her face, so your fingers rest on her jawbone and up toward her ear, and say pretty much anything in a soft voice: "I had a great time tonight" or "You're great" or even "Are you OK?" Turn your head toward hers as you speak and you simply can't get an easier approach for a kiss. It will happen so naturally, you won't even be able to remember who moved toward whom. In fact, when you've been a couple for several months, you'll probably argue with each other about who made the move.

The first kiss

Although the first kiss will tell her if she wants to go to bed with you, share her life with you, or even have your children, it doesn't have to be a perfect kiss in terms of technique. Nervous anticipation can cause you both to make jerky movements, and navigating your way around a new lover's nose, lips, and teeth can also take getting used to. But it's highly unlikely she'll be blaming you if your teeth crash together, your lips are slightly off-center, or you can't quite coordinate your tongue movements—she's far more likely to blame herself, so don't worry about it.

How to kiss

Once the initial lip landing has taken place, however clumsy, it's time to enjoy the kiss. Many men are too nervous to take time exploring a woman's lips, her tongue and face—but that's exactly what you need to do right now so that this kiss begins to feel amazing. Darting your tongue in and out like a lizard is a no-no; swirling her tongue firmly round and round using yours is another; keeping your tongue in your mouth is also a mistake.

Here's what to do. First, imagine that kissing this woman is your only goal, you don't need to feel her breasts or have sex with her because you find her lips and tongue so amazing that you could just do it forever. If you can give her this impression with your kiss, she's yours. Now let your lips meet, kiss, let her open her mouth, then allow your tongue a little way into her mouth, then part your lips a little further, exploring her tongue with yours more fully. Always move away very slightly every now and again so that you can both breathe, and try not to block off her entire mouth with yours—you're not trying to give her mouth-to-mouth, and it's far sexier to let your lips and tongue meet, and move around each other.

Try not to get hooked on having your tongue hung up inside her mouth: too many men forget to punctuate their tongue swordplay with closed or partially closed kissing. If you stick at open-mouthed kissing for too long, it begins to feel very boring, as well as tiring. Stopping at regular intervals helps to calm you both enough that you'll be able to fully appreciate kissing each other, rather than just feeling nervous, and it also feels affectionate and sexy.

Practicing

Get hold of a very ripe peach or mango and take a bite, then kiss and lick the flesh without breaking even the smallest piece off but while still getting a taste of the juice. That's how you should kiss a woman. And if you tell her kissing her is like eating delicious, sweet fruit, you'll earn extra points for an original compliment, too.

Breathing stops are like commas in your kissing sentences—without them the sentence, and the kiss, become labored and less pleasurable. It's not necessary to break away from her; take a deep breath then dive back in instead. Use the breathing space as an opportunity to kiss her even more gently or to look into her eyes or to kiss her on the side of her lips, her nose, wherever. This creates variety as well as letting you both get a bit of much-needed oxygen to those excitedly pumping hearts.

Continuing the kiss

It's impossible to overemphasize: you can't kiss a woman for too long. If she wants to move things forward and you've been kissing for a long time, she'll let you know—and it's far more flattering to have a woman undo her own top for you than to have her slap your hand or brusquely move it from her breast because she wasn't ready to take it to the next stage. And remember that women, like men, love to be teased. One of the biggest turn-ons for women is for a man to be very attracted to her, to be passionate but to hold back a little, making her want him even more. You'd be surprised to discover how many shy kitten-like women turn into tigers when they're teased a little.

There are times for hard, powerful kissing and times for soft, gentle kissing. If you're in a spontaneous and sweaty clinch in an alley, in a club toilet, or up against the wall of a corridor outside your apartment, then hot and heavy is probably the way to go. But as a general rule, soft, explorative kissing and touching is going to arouse her far more.

This isn't just due to women being soft and sensitive—far from it, she may well be shouting "Harder!" at you later—no, this is about nerve endings. Nerves respond more effectively to very gentle touching than they do to a firm touch. Test your own responses like this: using a pen-lid or a spoon, whichever is handiest, move it over the back of your hand only just touching the hairs on it. Feel that? Now press firmly over the same area. No tingles there. Enough said.

You're probably thinking, "How can I win?" Too hard and she won't enjoy it, too soft and she'll think you're a wuss. But by too soft I mean with no effort. Your lips can be soft but they need to meld with hers so that all those nerve endings get titillated.

Your tongue needn't be a hard rod of steel as it thrusts into her mouth like a sexual metaphor, but if it lies limp and lifeless in the bottom of her mouth, she's going to wonder if she forgot to spit her chewing gum out earlier! Again, use the ripe peach or mango to get the right tongue tension. If your tongue is so hard it's poking holes in the flesh of the peach you need to soften up a little; if you're barely managing to lick off any juice, it's too soft.

Unless you're both already tearing at each other's clothes, this kind of very passionate, dramatic kissing style is best avoided for first kisses. By diving in and going for full explorative thrusts with your tongue, you'll give her the impression you'll be like that in bed, too. She'll imagine a guy who won't bother with foreplay and will penetrate as soon as her clothes are off, thrusting until he's done. And that means you're going home alone.

Kiss first, touch later

Kissing is the most erotic thing you can do to a woman. Heading straight for the money—that is, her breasts or between her legs—is like eating your dinner before you've even sat down at the table.

Plus, her lips are an erogenous zone to compare easily with her breasts. Because lips are also used to identify food and are therefore essential for day-to-day survival, five of the twelve cranial nerves that affect brain function are involved when you kiss. Kissing her is a sure fire route to getting her fully aroused and wanting sex—then it'll be her grabbing your hand to put it between her legs.

Making it more than a kiss

Kissing is about so much more than your lips and tongue—it's about your eyes, your torso and, most importantly, your hands. Cupping your hands around her face as you kiss her makes her feel loved and adored; slipping your hand around the back of her head and sliding your hands into the hair at the nape of her neck will give her shivers of pleasure; and sliding one hand sexily right into the small of her back as you pull her waist toward you will make her feel dominated as well as womanly. Put your hand just below her hip so that your thumb is almost, very nearly touching the outer area of her pubic region, and that teasing effect will have her wanting you even more. Slide your hand up the side of her body, keeping your hand further toward the back of her body with just your thumb close to her breast and let it graze the outside of her breasts as you do so, and all the nerve endings in her breasts will be alert and at the ready. Take her, she's yours.

Kissing turn-offs

Oh dear. Bad breath is the number-one turn-off when it comes to kissing. And when you consider that women are assessing you as a potential mate based on your scent, it's not hard to imagine why: your bad breath says bad diet, bad hygiene, bad health. Don't bother asking friends if your breath smells—most will lie to save your ego. Instead, lick the inside of your wrist. Let it dry and then smell the patch. If it reeks, so does your breath.

Aside from brushing and flossing your teeth regularly, tongue scraping is one of the most effective ways to reduce bad breath. A lot of bacteria collect at the back of your tongue so removing them may help your kissing problems. If in any doubt, visit a dental hygienist who can give your entire mouth a once over.

And drink, drink, drink. No, not beer—water. Not only does this flush your system, helping your body remove toxins that could be causing bad smells, it moistens your mouth and throat so that bacteria are less likely to get a hold.

One final thought to throw into the mix: in a survey of the female staff of four major U.S. women's magazines, a massive 19.4 percent said they liked it when their man smelled of scotch. Worth a shot?

Spit happens

If you're kissing passionately and tongues are involved, there's likely to be a little bit of dribble somewhere on both of you. The key is not to insult her by wiping your mouth obviously and instead to take the responsibility: move away from her face, gently take her chin in your hand, and say, "Sorry," as you gently wipe away any moisture from her lips. Touch her lips and look at them as you do so—this is incredibly sexy—then, as if you're so turned on by looking at her luscious lips that you can't help it, kiss her again. She'll feel like you care, and are a gentleman, but also that you find her irresistible—an incredible turn-on.

Timing and Locations

Where and when you do it can change an average kiss into a phenomenal one. I've picked out some times and places that will have her weak at the knees with just a simple peck on the lips.

In bad weather

Films are to blame for this one. Script writers have romantic couples kissing in the most uncomfortable and awkward of situations for good reason: if you feel so strongly about each other, and want to kiss each other so badly that you're willing to get soaked to the bone, or blown away by gale-force winds, it shows that your desire is utterly and totally powerful, over-whelming even. And that's sexy as well as romantic. To make it extra special—and probably the kind of moment she'll tell her friends about, write in her diary, or remind you of when you've been married for ten years—take your coat/jacket/newspaper and put it over your heads as you kiss her, laughing. You'll be creating your own cinematic moment.

Other locations or moments that work well are: at a busy train station (especially through a train window or door), in a field with long grass, on a windswept beach, on top of a mountain, or in the snow (and if it's cold, always wrap her up in your own coat while you're still wearing it, so she's tucked inside—it's cozy and gets her very close).

Just like the movies

A lot of the things that women find most romantic are based on things they've seen in films. And more than standard lip or neck kissing, kissing on the forehead always indicates that the leading man truly loves his leading lady. It's protective and sweet—which, if you've just had an amazing night of passionate sex, will seal the deal for future encounters. Similarly, kissing her on her shoulder if she's wearing a strappy top is an erotic move you can get away with in public and it'll make her feel really sexy.

Reunited with a kiss

You've just arrived back from a trip and you're in the middle of a crowd—perfect timing for a heartfelt kiss. This is a tricky one, as you might not want to get in the way of the crowds and your mind's probably on things like where the car is, your luggage, and so on. But now, more than ever, you need to give her a few moments of your time. It's important to look into her eyes before and after you kiss her, rather than immediately looking up to see where the exit is or if someone's stolen your suitcase. Focus on the moment—kiss her slowly and gently, look into her eyes, and then say, "It's so good to see you. Come on, let's go home." Fail to say hello properly like this, and you'll be paying the price for the rest of the night, maybe even the week. She needs to know how you feel immediately; otherwise she'll be hurt and that means it'll be harder for her to open up and relax with you, let alone get turned on enough to make love to you later.

Meeting your friends

Public displays of affection can be disgusting or sweet. There's no need to swirl your tongue around her larynx in order to show her you care; a simple kiss on the shoulder while you're out is more than enough, better even, than a kiss on the mouth. It's your subtle way of telling her you're thinking of her, even though you may have been talking about football or baseball for the last 30 minutes, that you appreciate her being there, and, most importantly, that you're not afraid for your friends to know how important she is to you. All these things count as major brownie points—you'll reap the rewards manifold later.

Recreating teenage excitement

To recreate that teenage excitement, kiss her when you're somewhere it can't go any further. Kissing for the sake of kissing is what makes it exciting again. Do it on a street corner, on the train, or in the kitchen while your guests are waiting in the dining room.

There really, truly is no better way to rev up the excitement levels in a relationship.

Real Girls Tell All

LINDA describes the kiss that led to her marriage:

"We were sitting on a bench on top of a hill. It was a hot, humid day, overcast but sticky. We'd just walked quite a way so we were both a bit sweaty really, and so we sat quite far apart and just gazed out at the view. I had some water and we drank some, then suddenly rain started pouring down. At first, we both panicked a bit, not really knowing where to go or run to. But then we started laughing and we both stood up to turn our bodies toward the rain. He took my hand and I can't really remember how, but we ended up kissing. The rain stopped almost as quickly as it started, but we carried on kissing and kissing and kissing...and now we're married."

GAIL describes her best kiss:

"He had the softest lips I'd ever seen. It was like dipping your lips in whipped cream, and I felt like I melted when we first kissed. My eyes shut and it really felt as though nothing existed, like my body had disappeared. I really wasn't even aware of myself. He had this way of opening my lips with his tongue, ever so gently, and then moving it along the inside of my lips and the outside, too, as if he wanted to taste me. He'd kiss the corners of my mouth and all around the edges and he'd make me feel like the most special woman in the world. If only his personality had been as good as his kiss, I might have stuck with it!'"

SUZY describes the best kissing technique:

"I like it passionate and powerful. I want a man to push me up against a wall and press his lips against mine—then I know how much he wants me. I want his hands to be on my body, behind my head pulling my face in toward his, on my back to pull me in really tight. I want him to bite on my neck and shoulders, to tug on my lips with his mouth. That's what I call a passionate kiss."

3

Breasts

Soft, round pillows with a darkened bud at the center, breasts are undeniably eye-catching, but more important is the fact that the way you approach and touch them will dictate whether or not a woman gets aroused...and whether you get any further.

In this chapter I will tell you exactly what is going on in her mind when you admire her breasts, how best to compliment her on them, her physiological responses to different types of touch, and her own attitude toward them. You can use this information at any stage of a relationship. And whatever you do or say, you'll know what's going through her mind.

Admiring Her Breasts

On a good day, her puppies are like a great lover—
they make her feel wanted, sexy, and get her wetter
between the legs than anything else. But even when
she's feeling good about her breasts, your reaction to
the sight of them could elicit a bad response. Make
sure you get it right by following these guidelines.

Why she *really* wears revealing clothing

Pink lace peeking out over the top of her jeans, a
flash of red as she leans over the counter, or a black
bra strap that seems to keep falling off her shoulder—whatever the titillating vista she's presenting you
with, it's highly likely she's aware of it. Women may
claim they wear stockings or lacy underwear to please
themselves, but it's an argument that holds up only
in certain situations. When there's a good chance the
top of a stocking, a G-string or a bra will be seen
by others—that is, if the skirt is very short, the jeans
very low-cut or the top transparent—it's for others'
benefit, too.

Flashing a bit of color to draw the attention of the
opposite sex is something many other animals—as well
as humans—do. The bower bird of New Guinea and
Australia creates a nest and decorates it with colored

flowers and fruit; baboons flash their colorful rears at each other; and squids put on a fantastic light-and-color show for whoever they're hoping to entwine tentacles with. There's absolutely no guarantee that her display is meant for you; however, it could be that she just wants to feel sexually attractive in general. That said, if you're on a date or having a drink with her, that showy bra is definitely a visual cue—take heed, and later, you could find yourself entangled in her straps.

Unfortunately, it gets more complicated because if she catches you staring at her breasts—however beautifully they may be presented—she may well feel offended. This might be surprising, illogical even, considering what I've just said about her underwear, but looking at breasts is like looking at the sun: a glance won't hurt you, but stare too long and you'll suffer permanent damage.

Here's the logic: firstly, women have better peripheral vision than men, so all that time you were looking when you thought she couldn't tell, she could—and you were looking way too long; secondly, she may not want you to stare at her breasts—it might be in aid of some other lucky fella; thirdly, if she does catch you looking—which she's likely to if you keep ogling—

she'll feel obliged to respond in a negative manner so as not to look like a tart or a tease. The result? She feels embarrassed and annoyed, and you get verbally slapped around the face. And that hurts.

Going topless

If your girlfriend is one of the many women who love an even tan, try to encourage her to fake it instead. The drying effect of the sun will further reduce the skin's elasticity, making her breasts far more likely to sag in later life. Tanning also creates that leathery, crinkly skin effect—not attractive on any body. And because the skin on the bony area between the breasts is so thin, she's far more likely to burn, too—which puts her at greater risk of skin cancer. Hand her the fake bronzer and you'll be enjoying her fabulous breasts for far longer.

When her nipples say hello

Nipples, just like your penis and her clitoris and vaginal lips, are made up of tissue that swells up in response to stimuli. But don't be fooled into thinking that the sight of you still wet after your gym session has caused her body to respond in this way. Yes, the stimuli can be something very sexy, like your sweaty buff body at the gym, but it's far more likely to be a sudden cold blast from the air-conditioner; or it could simply be the feel of her top's material rubbing over her nipples. What's more, some women's nipples are on permanent red alert—and for this reason alone, it's not a good idea to rely on her erect nipples as an indicator of sexual attraction. If you're kissing or touching her, however, and her rosebuds begin to take the shape of torpedo missiles, her body is responding to what you're doing—so keep doing it!

Complimenting her breasts ⚡

Those big pendulous globes—you can't get enough of them. You could spend hours nuzzling them, rubbing your hands over them, squeezing them…loving them. That's all well and good, but, unfortunately, the larger her breasts are, the more likely it is that she won't get the same enjoyment out of it that you do.

Small breasts are more sensitive to temperature and touch than larger breasts, purely because the nerve endings that are in the breast are spread over a far smaller area. On larger breasts the skin is stretched and the feather-light touching that makes one small-breasted woman squeal with pleasure may not even register on a larger lady.

But that's not to say they should be ignored; far from it, but it is a question of adapting your approach to each woman's personality and her feelings about her breasts. The average woman's breast size is 36C—this is a good handful, but certainly not what most would class as large. For some large-breasted women, men's focus on this one part of their body becomes rather predictable, which makes it boring. They may feel defined by the size of their breasts, something that could make them feel uncomfortable about the undue attention you give them.

No matter how many times men say they prefer the real thing, women continue to crave perfectly round new—fake—breasts. Get rid of her insecurities by telling her exactly what you love about hers. Focus on an individual aspect of them—how great they look when she's on top, how they move under her T-shirt or how amazing they look in that dress/bra/top. Tailoring your compliment to her makes it seem far more genuine and also appears more off-the-cuff and natural. Those are the compliments she'll remember.

Knowing Her Breasts

Even if you've spent quite a lot of time fondling, licking, sucking, and generally playing with your girlfriend's lady pillows, there are still secrets to be revealed about them. Here are the things you may not yet have learned about her feelings about them and their physiological responses to your touch.

How she touches her breasts

Did you think she didn't? What would you do if you had a pair? Feel them, of course! If she loves the sensation of your hands, lips, and tongue on her fleshy orbs, then the chances are that when she masturbates, she plays with them to get herself to climax.

Breasts, along with the fingertips, face, and genital area, are the most sensitive parts of the body. These areas are packed with nerve endings so that even the slightest whisper will be felt on the skin. Ask her to describe how she plays with her breasts when you're not around—even if she just shows you by guiding your hand over them or by telling you over the phone, if she's comfortable with that. How she plays solo will give you the best indication of how to bring her to climax during sex. Don't miss your clue.

How to look at her naked breasts

If she turns out the light every time you get close to getting naked, it could be that she feels uncomfortable about how her breasts look. Because breasts often grow very quickly during puberty, the skin sometimes doesn't have time to adapt and the elastin beneath the skin's surface breaks, leaving white lines—stretch marks. You may have them on your bum, on your knees, thighs or even your biceps if you've built up muscle in a short space of time. Many women have them on their breasts.

You won't have noticed this in magazine photographs because photographers use "soft boxes," which are lights with a large piece of special material that helps diffuse light, creating smooth and attractive-looking skin and lines. These soft boxes are available at professional photography shops and are a good way to make her feel more relaxed in your bedroom—but you can also inquire in your local lighting shop, asking for soft-light bulbs or a diffusing lampshade, which will have the same effect.

There are other ways to use flattering lighting in your bedroom as well: candles are the obvious choice and they provide an even, soft skin tone and hide blemishes on both you and her, but you can also buy low-wattage bulbs with a tint of orange-brown or pink to show skin off to its best advantage.

And once you've got her comfortable with being naked with the light on, take care with how much time you spend simply looking at her breasts. Being studied can make a woman feel beautiful, but it's also just as likely to make her feel self-conscious. In fact, she may be aware of "imperfections" in her breasts that you don't even see. Just as your balls are unique—you'd know them apart in photos probably—so are her breasts. Statistically, it's likely her left breast is bigger than her right. Ask any honest woman you know, and it's virtually guaranteed she'll even have one she prefers to the other. Her nipples are also different from each other—in shape, texture, and color. And some women have an inverted nipple, where, instead of a button, there's a slit. This isn't a problem, but it can be disconcerting and embarrassing for her.

The way in which you look at her breasts and nipples is just as important as how long you spend doing it. If you are looking at her nipples or breasts, then kissing them or fondling them, she knows it's in adoration; if you spend a long time staring without saying or doing something to let her know you love them, she'll feel far more uncomfortable. Instead of looking closely, try shutting your eyes and explore her body with your tongue, your lips, and your hands.

When your compliments fall on deaf ears

So you'd like to get your hands on her breasts and you think a good way to get there is to compliment her on them. She gives you a look that would cause a wasp to shudder. Why? Because she thinks she knows what you're up to, that you're just saying it to be nice. And that's because when women say they love your "cuddly" midriff, your "squidgy" bum and your cute chubby cheeks, they're just saying it to be nice. They don't want to hurt you with the truth: they'd far rather you were fit, healthy, and looked great. So when you say you like her curves, she thinks you're lying, too. Only you're not. Are you?

Her breast is made up of adipose tissue—that's fat to you—and connective tissue. The mammary glands are actually inside this fatty tissue. Connective tissue—called Cooper's ligaments in the breast—provide most of the support for this extra fatty weight and over time, with ageing, naturally lose their strength. The ligaments can, however, prematurely lose elasticity and strength through impact sports such as running, lack of support and fluctuating weight. That can lead to her feeling her breasts aren't as pert or firm as she thinks they should be.

If she's a regular dieter, it's likely her breasts aren't what they used to be. One of the problems with women's obsession with dieting is that it ruins the skin's elasticity—if it is continually swinging from being stretched, then shrunk again, like a rubber band, it eventually snaps. That's what stretch marks are—where the collagen under the skin has effectively snapped—and they're often caused by dieting or weight gain, and also pregnancy. Once the skin loses this elasticity, her breasts will sag—an eventuality that will make her far more paranoid than a couple of extra pounds.

What you can do is encourage her to exercise rather than diet. Because diets are often quite drastic, the weight-loss—and often the gain that comes once the diet is dropped—is so sudden that the skin simply doesn't have time to respond. Gentle exercise will use up extra calories and, over time, she'll lose the weight she'd like to. And while she's there, join her—then you can lose that cuddly midriff, too.

Why do her breasts look firmer sometimes?
They look juicy and bitable because blood is flooding into the area, making them swollen and feeling bruised—a little bit like when you strain an ankle or

your wrist. And just as you would rather no one gave your sprained wrist a sexy squeeze, so she'd rather you'd kept your hands off. And in a cruel twist of fate—just as her breasts swell up to a third of a size bigger, just before and during her period, you want to touch them and she wants you to steer well clear.

There is, however, a possible solution. Use a lubricant and go gently. Getting her breasts lubed up means that your touch won't pull and tug at the swollen tissue; instead, your hands will glide over her shining love-pillows. And what's more, she's actually likely to have an even more intense orgasm just before or during her period, so she may even thank you for the breast massage.

If she's just had a baby, her breasts will also swell—but far more than half a cup size. This is what happens when a woman breastfeeds her newborn. And although her breasts might look deliciously plump and touchable, the purpose of her soft protrusions changes dramatically and her feelings about them change, too.

Some men fantasize about suckling from a mother's breasts, but it's pretty much guaranteed that this fantasy is not a new mother's idea of fun. Milk is drained from the mammary glands inside the breast, out into tiny holes in the nipple—called lactiferous ducts—and out to get to her baby's mouth. But the milk doesn't flow like a tap that just gets turned on once the baby's mouth locks on—no, it involves sucking and, if the baby's teething, a bit of inadvertent nibbling, too. The constant sucking and moisture often causes new mothers' nipples to get dry and sore; sometimes they also crack and bleed. A good reason to leave her nipples alone at this time.

Buying her underwear DON'T !

Her bra says a lot about how she feels about her fleshy protrusions and what you buy her or want her to wear can affect how she feels about you, too. You need to find out exactly how bras work, which styles suit different shapes and sizes, and what her preferences are before you buy.

First, cast your mind back to art class—what's the complementary color of red? Green, of course. And this basic fact means that unless your girlfriend has the deepest, darkest skin, red lingerie will make her look pale and slightly green. And only the Incredible Hulk can get away with that skin tone. If you're not sure what her skin tone is, best to play it safe and leave red well alone.

Her dislike of red undies is more than skin-deep, however, it's also about character. Red is one of nature's showiest colors—it says lust, passion, and danger. But it's also a color that is seen as a statement of intent—the woman who wears red to a wedding is a harlot looking for a show-down; the sexy lady with the red bra on is cheap or easy; and the teenage girl with red stilettos on is "out on the prowl." It's a real shame that this is the case, because red has this power precisely because it's such a sexy color.

But the fact remains that there are very few women who feel comfortable in a red bra and panties. But beyond comfort, this is about how she is perceived by you—she wants to surprise you with her sassiness in bed, her wild lust and her red-hot passion; by presenting her with a gift of red underwear, it's as though you're telling her you think she's cheap, or, even worse, that you'd like her to be, even though she's not.

So unless you know she'd like red underwear—that is, she's actually asked for some or wears it regularly—just don't buy her any. Instead, if it's your favorite under-wear color or if you want to encourage her to wear it, get her black underwear with just a tiny detail in red: a bow at the front of a pair of black French panties, trimming on a navy G-string, or the lace at the top of a white bra.

The basics of bras

Admittedly, buying her underwear is a minefield, so make sure you're au fait with the basics. Here's a brief lesson in lingerie to avoid losing a limb: the figure on her bra refers to two things—her cup size (how much you can fit in your hand) and her chest circumference (how far you can wrap your arms around her). So a pair of DD breasts won't appear quite as big if they're on a woman with a 44in chest, because the fleshy bit is spread over a larger area; likewise, a pair of C-cup breasts will look more than ample on a 28in chest.

It sounds fairly straightforward, but there's more: some brands will differ widely from others. Just as with your underpants, sizes differ between one designer and another—you might fit into a large pair with one, and need an extra-large in another. Ask a shop assistant for help with buying her a bra or do some research on the Internet—or if you want no-nonsense accurate advice, ask her sister or best friend.

If you want to get her something as a surprise, go through her laundry basket—in that you'll find her most comfortable, regular bras. These are probably the ones that are the right size—they fit well, so they're comfy. But these are also likely to be the ones she doesn't wear to feel sexy—for that, you need to go digging in her underwear drawers. If there's a lot of black lace in there, it means that's her preference; likewise white, turquoise, cerise, and so on. Be aware that even with extensive bra size research and careful shopping, the bra you buy her may not fit. Like shoes, a size in one brand may be perfect; in another, painful.

And if you're still in doubt, ask her best friend's advice. Unlike you, women discuss underwear with each other, so she'll know exactly what to get. Plus, you'll gain instant recognition as "great boyfriend material" from her peer group. She'll be grinning from ear to ear and so will you.

Touching Her Breasts

The way you get physical with her orbs of pleasure can make the difference between sending her into a state of quivering arousal or shuddering with disgust, or, even worse, pain. Read on to find out what she likes, what she doesn't, and how to improve your technique.

The bra's off

A breast is like a dartboard—you instinctively head for the bull's eye, the nipple, because it stands out visually and physically. But that approach won't win you maximum points in the mating game.

Exploration is always the best way to get maximum arousal—for you and for her, so try not to neglect parts of her body. The sides of her breasts are incredibly ticklish—and that means there are lots of nerve endings there, so don't starve them of your touch. Next time you're in bed, ask her to put her arms up beside her head, then trace the back of your hand along the heavy curve of her breasts on both sides. Now do the same with your fingertips and then your *and tops* tongue. This is virtually guaranteed to have her squirming with pleasure.

Once you've spent some quality time with the sides of her breasts, slowly make your way into the center. Lack of speed is key here—you're building up to hitting the most sensitive part: her nipple. If you take your time, letting her work up a powerful arousal, when you do let your lips or fingers lightly brush her nipples, it will be the most exquisite sensation for her. Her back will arch as she thrusts her chest toward you—and you'll feel like the breast man. And you are.

And when you're applying your hands, think about how much pressure to use. The breast stroke is a great way to begin—it's simply feather-light touching. Gentle touch actually stimulates more of the skin's nerve endings than a grope. That's why it feels so good to her.

This isn't always the case, however. There are times when, in the heat of the moment, she wants to feel the power of your hands on her body, but when it comes to turning her on, getting her into the mood, you can't beat the light touch. Think of her breasts as ripe fruit and treat them accordingly—too hard and she'll bruise.

Using your mouth

Licking her nipple like it's a lollipop can send her into a state of total ecstasy. The nipple, just like the clitoris, feeds into orgasm-inducing neurons in the brain, and some women are able to climax through breast stimulation alone. In each nipple are receptors called Meissner's corpuscles, cells that are able to adjust to different stimuli—this could include your warm, moist mouth, a frozen grape rubbed gently over the area, or even warm oil.

Take care when attempting nibbling, biting, or sucking hard—these can feel fantastic on her breasts and nipples, but, just like when she's down on you, nibbling, biting, and sucking your manhood hard, there's a fine line between fantastically erotic and just downright painful.

One of the most common complaints from women with regard to nipple playing is that men treat them like cooker controls—they think if they twist hard, they'll up the sexual temperature, but that's not how it works. The more sexual tension you can build, the more explosive the climax will be—jumping into bed with muscular fingers at the ready is more likely to turn her cold.

Use your own body as a pain barometer—how hard could you pull at the skin of your testicles, or squeeze and tweak the sensitive glans, the head of your penis? Approach her breasts—especially her nipples—with the same level of gentle care. And gauge her reactions: if she pushes her breasts into your hands when you're very gently swirling your fingertip around the edges, try pressing on them with your thumbs; if she's still thrusting herself harder against your hands, turn up the volume a little. Just take it slowly, gradually building up any pressure you apply—that way she can let you know when to go further and when to slow back down.

If she enjoys her nipples or breasts being very firmly stimulated, it's a good idea to agree on a code so that you know when you're being too firm, causing her unpleasant pain. Biting—often quite violent—is a fairly common element of mating between many different types of animals. But you really don't want to make the same mistakes that some animals do: the male mink, for example, sometimes accidentally pierces his partner's brain, killing her. That's one type of heart-stopping sex! To avoid overdoing it, use a word you wouldn't ever use in bed: "Coventry" or "spider" or something like that. Yes, you'll feel a bit silly, but not as silly as you'd both feel if she suffered an injury from your overzealous loving.

The breath trick

This is one of the easiest but most effective techniques to use on any part of her body, but it works best on her breast and nipple. Once you've licked or sucked, simply pull back your head and blow gently over the area. What this does is take her skin's temperature from warm—from her own natural body temperature and from your warm licking—to cool, when the moisture from your sucking evaporates. And this makes her nerve endings respond, increasing sensitivity to whatever you next decide to do to that area—stroke, kiss, or even gently nibble.

When it's good to get more hands-on

Men tend to focus on a woman's nipples if she has small breasts, which is a shame because she may well enjoy having the entire breast massaged. Bee-sting breasts are often more sensitive to touch than bigger breasts, and therefore, hold the key to getting her extremely turned on, extremely quickly.

If you don't find her smaller breasts as visually stimulating as larger ones, get some scaffolding put up. Not outside the house, but underneath her breasts. A balconette bra is perfect for a woman with smaller breasts as it pushes them upwards and leaves the upper area clear for viewing. Don't worry, she won't suspect that you want her breasts to look or feel bigger—balconette bras are just one of the many styles available. If she keeps the bra on during sex, you can touch and fondle the fleshy upper area and nipple. Once she's got support, the only way is up.

Real Girls Tell All

SARAH on having a big pair of breasts:

"Both my boyfriend and I love my boobs. They're fairly big—I'm a double D—and I've always had lots of attention, from both women and men, because of them. Women sometimes come up and ask me if they're real—I always let them have a feel so that they know they're genuine. I'd never want fake ones. They look hard; it must be like fondling a pair of soccer balls. Mine feel more like balloons filled with water, firmer than that, but they jiggle like balloons when I walk fast.

"My boyfriend likes to come over mine. I put my arms together so he can slide himself between them and then he pushes himself up and down— it's funny how much he loves it, but I don't mind because he's one of the most caring men I've ever been with. He always, always makes me come first. "Ladies first," he always says. I like that, and it means he always gets a smile as well as sex. You want both, don't you?"

GINA on playing with hers:

"I absolutely love playing with my tits. They're only small, and to be honest, my ex-boyfriends have never paid them enough attention. It's like they think that because they're small, they're not as important, but if a man wants to get me really wet, he's got to play with them.

"When I masturbate, I do it in front of a mirror, just so I can look at my tits. It really turns me on to see them. I put on a push-up bra and just seeing them gives me a shiver in between my legs. I used to think that was a bit weird and that I should get turned on by looking at a guy's bits, not my own tits, but I don't care—it's just what does it for me.

"My all-time favorite is to wear a push-up bra and use baby lotion on them so they feel really slippery. They look so good like that, all glistening and bouncy. I imagine my man is the one touching them; he's grabbing and squeezing them. It feels so good, and it looks so good, I come easily every time.

"My current boyfriend knows how much I love to have them touched, and I wear my push-up in bed with him. He knows it's what makes me come and he gets off on that, so it works for both of us. And it's definitely made me more satisfied in bed. We do it all the time!

TANYA on getting her breasts wet:

"When I lie in the bath, my boobs look absolutely amazing. I sometimes wish that I had a much bigger bath—one that was conducive to sex—because then my husband could enjoy them as much as I do when I'm alone in there.

"I usually put a generous amount of foaming bubble bath in—then I slide my naked body into the hot water. Even feeling water all around me is somehow luxurious and sexy, but the foam makes it feel really special—the bubbles fizz and pop on my skin and, as the foam begins to disappear, my nipples begin to show through. When the cold air hits them, they immediately pop out and say hi to the world. The deep pink of the area around my little popped-out raspberries looks glossy and shiny, and full of color—they look delicious, I wish I could reach them with my mouth to suck on them.

"Because of the support of the bath water, the flesh of my breast is pushed upwards. They look round and healthy and ready to be touched, almost as though they're thrust outwards in anticipation. By now all the foam is gone and I play with my nipples by moving my body down into the water, so my breasts are fully covered—my nipples some-times go down a little; then I rise up, pushing my breasts out into the colder outside air, and my raspberries pop out again.

"I tease myself like this for a while and then I slowly trace my fingers from just above my pubic hair, ever so lightly touching my skin, and work my way to just below my breasts. I run my finger along underneath and to the sides, anywhere but the nipple itself. By now I'm arching my back, desperate to home in on the nipple, to feel the explosion of sensation there, but I keep teasing myself as I know it will be all the more satisfying when I get there.

"I move my middle fingers gently onto my nipples and it makes me gasp—I'm pushing toward my fingers, as though they belong to someone else, like I am not fully in control, and then I swirl my fingertips over and around them. It feels just fantastic and it's why I love to take baths."

4

Sex positions

Men place far too much emphasis on sex positions—I blame the *Kama Sutra* for that. Flipping a woman over like a pancake, leaping across the bedroom like a frog, or other "new" positions that result in colliding knees and elbows or your toes dangling in her face are not going to impress her. Your angle of approach is important, but it really won't make you good in bed. What it can do, however, is improve your, or her, physical experience of sex. Considered positioning can make a wide vagina feel tighter and a penis feel longer, and it makes both of you have more intense orgasms. Every sex position range has its plus and minus points—enjoy exploring them all.

Her On Top

It's the position most likely to bring her to orgasm and it affords you some great views, but there's more to this than meets the eye.

It's not always good for you

Have you ever found that she gets on top then, once she's orgasmed, seems to lose enthusiasm? Well, welcome to reality—women can be selfish, too. And if her taking hold of the reins means you get left behind, she's not going to be shedding any tears. Blame your forefathers, your brothers, and your male contemporaries, because the chances are she's heard about and had a lot of sex where men don't care a bean for a woman's orgasm. And so she knows to grab the orgasm opportunity with both hands whenever it arises. What's more, once she's come, her body releases the same chemicals your body does when you've come—the ones that make you feel sleepy and lethargic. That's why her enthusiastic jiving on your penis becomes more like a slow samba, leaving you with little chance of an orgasm unless you change positions.

Something for her to learn

To try to aim for a simultaneous orgasm in the her-on-top position, she needs to learn more about her climax. She can teach herself to hold back and discover how to control the point of orgasm by practicing when she masturbates. Women, like men, tend to try to get to the end goal as quickly as they're able, but taking herself close to the edge of orgasm, then pulling back, and repeating the process will teach her how to control her climax and may even lead to more intense orgasms. It also means she can control her climax until you're close to yours, making it a lot easier for you both to enjoy an orgasm in the same few minutes.

She won't get on top?

Sitting astride a man, bringing herself to orgasm as he watches, is really putting herself out there—she's never more exposed and natural. That can be fantastic and amazing, and, thankfully, it is for a lot of women, but for those who dislike their bodies, it can just be unnerving and unpleasant. Being on top means taking centerstage—not only is she in control of her own orgasm but she's also there to make sex great for you, and to look good for you. If she hates the way her breasts look, thinks they're too jiggly or has a complex about her belly, for example, she's likely to feel like she can't really relax and let go in this position, making it highly unlikely she'll orgasm.

You can't change the way a woman feels about her body with a couple of compliments, but it'll go some way to making her reconsider how other people see her body. The way you touch her breasts or belly is really important—a woman can sense more about how much you love her breasts by the way you tenderly kiss them, caress them, and admire them while doing so, than if you simply tell her they're great. Combine both verbal compliments and hands-on physical compliments for the best results. Used repetitively, compliments will eventually make her believe that you think her body is fabulous, and gradually her inner cowgirl will be ready to saddle up.

That's not her problem, but she still won't get on top

She may have deep-seated emotional issues with getting on top. If that's the case, and she really doesn't like it, it's tough but sometimes a woman simply isn't in the mood for being the star of the show. The cowgirl position is fantastic sexy fun but it doesn't have the same tender intimacy as missionary, say, where your faces are close together at all times and your bodies are touching from head to toe. But she can still achieve that while on top in two ways: what I call the flatliner and the bargirl.

For the flatliner, she needs to be well lubricated, so have a bottle or tube to hand. Smearing your chest and her inner thighs with lube, she lies on top of you, putting your manhood in between her thighs. She then slides up and down, squeezing her thighs on your penis as she does so—there's no penetration, but you should feel a similar amount of friction (if not more!) than when you're inside her. This is a fantastic way to give her vaginal lips a lot of stimulation, too. And many women find it easier to orgasm that way.

For the bargirl, you'll need some kind of stool or chair. You sit on it while she straddles you. She's on top, giving you the view you want, with her in full control, but you still enjoy the intimacy of being close face to face. It's such a simple technique but is so effective at helping her to orgasm, as her clitoris gets more stimulation from your pelvis and abdomen and it allows her to push down on you while still being able to kiss and feel your chest against hers. Perfect.

Reversing the cowgirl position

Although this is a great position for you—you lie back and get a fantastic view of her rear and your penis thrusting inside her—it's unlikely she'll orgasm like this. Her clitoris doesn't get to bang up against your pelvis in this position, which can leave her wanting. But that's no excuse; she's got hands—she can use them! If she still needs encouragement, get a vibrating penis ring and put it on upside-down; that is, with the vibe toward your testicles. That'll have her sitting pretty happy for as long as the batteries hold out—meanwhile you get to enjoy the view of her rear as she mounts you.

We've done all that

Easy, cowboy, if you've done all the variations above, there are even more positions to try—more than could ever be covered in one book, even the *Kama Sutra*. For an unusual, yet very sexy position, try this: you sit semi-upright, propped up with lots of pillows and she clambers on top of you, facing your feet so that her back rests against your stomach, and slides you inside her. It's tricky to maneuver into, but it is possible if your penis is long enough, and this is one of the most sensuous positions. Your hands are free to come around the front and play with her breasts and her clitoris and, although she's on top, you share control and she feels very exposed but incredibly aroused by your wandering hands and the feeling of your penis inside her.

You On Top

Missionary sex is fabulous and totally underrated. I've talked to many women who say they love this position because they can feel and see their partner; men say the same. But it's not the easiest position for her to climax, so let's look at some ways you can improve on that.

Making her O your mission

Success here relies on you being shallow: her body isn't designed to orgasm with deep penetration—the majority of her nerve endings are in the lower third of her vaginal canal. To get an idea of how little sensation she has "up there," consider the cervical smear, a procedure during which cells are scraped from the cervix—and she doesn't even need an anesthetic. Now consider how she responds when you have a ragged fingernail and touch her vaginal lips or clitoris with it. See the difference? That is why deep thrusting, although potentially sexy, isn't what brings her to orgasm.

You can greatly enhance clitoral stimulation during missionary by changing your thrust technique. Rather than pulling out and in, slide yourself in and make hoops with your hips—circle and grind as you would if you were doing some seriously snake-hipped salsa moves on the dance floor. The point is to apply pressure to her clitoris with the upper part of the base of your penis and your pelvic bone. Maintain the same rhythm and keep going, kissing her neck or breasts as you do so. Don't expect her to orgasm quickly, or at all—just let her enjoy the sensation.

Giving her clitoris the attention it deserves

It's a greedy little bundle of nerves, the clitoris—and for some women, it simply craves your direct touch. You may be giving the grind and shallow thrust your best efforts and she's still unable to orgasm. So try employing one or both of these tools: a pillow and a vibrating penis ring. Putting a pillow under her bottom raises her pelvis toward yours, and puts the clitoris in a more exposed position. And a vibrating penis ring is a wonderful sex toy that slips over your manhood—it's stretchy so doesn't hurt or pinch—and directly stimulates her clitoris via a thumbnail-sized vibe at the top of the ring. Lord of the rings? You will be once you've tried it.

When she's too aroused

It's happened to most of us at one time or another— you're enjoying great sex, going at it, her juices are flowing and after a while, well, it doesn't feel quite as snug down there as it did at the start. It's a shame that a woman can become so aroused and wet that sensation is reduced for both of you, but lubrication does reduce friction to an extent. You slide easily in and out of her, which sounds great, but actually means there isn't all that much friction on your penis, and her vaginal walls barely seem to register your manhood's presence!

An easy, short-term solution is for her to use her fingers. She simply slides her hand down between your bodies and, with her fingers in a Victory-V shape, slots your penis in between the "V." She can even slide her fingers around the outside of her vaginal lips so that she's squeezing her lips tighter around your penis, too. Squeezing like this creates a sensation of a tight vaginal entrance while the base of her index finger will be perfectly positioned to put pressure on her clitoris. It's actually a fantastic way to get yourselves to orgasm.

Training for a tighter vagina

A long-term solution is for her to do Kegel exercises (squeezing her pelvic floor muscles) regularly. She can locate these muscles by noticing how she uses them to halt her urine flow when she goes to the toilet. Focusing on doing that will allow her to then clench that muscle wherever she is, on the toilet or on the train, in the office or in bed. Kegels can revolutionize your sex life. Not only do they tighten and tone, and grip a slimmer penis more tightly, but they can also give her more intense orgasms, too. There are lots of products on the market that exercise these muscles—pelvic toners, vaginal exercisers—see which ones work for her. Then, when you're having sex, she can use these muscles to increase the friction for both of you.

On All Fours

Great for making short or thin penises feel wider and longer, this versatile position isn't always her favorite, so let's look at ways to make it great for her, too.

Your penis is on the short side

If you're reading this, you're highly likely to be one of the many men who are wrong about their penis size. A man underestimating the size of his penis is like a woman overestimating the size of her behind—it's a classic and oft-repeated mistake. When urologists at a U.S. university asked men to estimate their penis size, they found that almost all got the figure wrong. The participants were pleasantly surprised to find that their magic wands were all bigger than their eyes had led them to believe. So, just for the record—the average erect penis measures between 5½in and 6½in; its girth is between 4½in and 5½in.

No, it really is on the short side!

OK, for the sake of argument let's just assume that you do in fact have a short or slim penis; doing it on all fours is a great way to extend yourself. It's not about you; it's a result of the angle of her body. Inside, her vaginal canal is directed more toward her back than her stomach—so in missionary, your penis fits just right; on all fours, your penis gets more friction on the top of the shaft, as well as on the head of the penis inside her. Similarly, if you're on top and her legs are slung over your shoulders, everything feels far tighter for you and her—especially if your penis is shorter. What happens is that the vaginal canal shortens (imagine a straightish tube that you bend into a U shape and you'll get an exaggerated idea of what happens when she puts her knees by her shoulders). And because the lower third of her vagina is massively engorged with blood when she's aroused, creating a barrel of spongy tissue, shortening the canal concentrates all that "sponge" into a smaller area, making the "tunnel" feel smaller.

She won't do doggy?

The very first time a woman is asked to go on all fours, she will undoubtedly wonder why the man she's in bed with would prefer to see the back of her. And, if you're new in bed together, steering clear of doggy-style might be a good idea, as it can feel impersonal when you're still getting to know and trust someone. Similarly, if you've been together for a long time and you insist on doing it on all fours every time, try to imagine how you'd feel if she always wanted to have sex in a position where she couldn't actually see you. And while I'm having a go at the doggy-style, consider this final blow: it's near impossible for her to have an orgasm in this position unless you lend a helping hand.

Making doggy a style she enjoys

To make sure she knows you love how she looks and that you adore her front and back, suggest doing it in front of a mirror. Not only does this create a visual feast for you, it gives her something—anything!—to look at. Otherwise it's hard for her to see anything but the bedspread unless she cranes her neck around to look at you. Fondle her breasts, her waist, and her neck as you have sex, and kiss her back and shoulders. And use your hands to help her to orgasm—that way her clitoris gets the stimulation it requires. Without help, your penis is thrusting in and out, giving her vaginal opening a lot of stimulation but never quite hitting on the clitoris, which simply isn't placed well for doggy-style stimulation. Another method is to provide her with a clitoral-bumper: pile cushions or pillows underneath her, in between her legs, so that each time you thrust, her clitoris and vaginal lips come into contact with the pile. Better still, strap a vibrator onto a pile of pillows and place them beneath her. Piles have never been sexier.

Side By Side

Perfect for lazy Sundays, doing it side by side can be one of the most intimate and erotic positions. It can also be frustratingly tricky and unsatisfying. Here's how to make sure you get it right.

Getting the right positioning

You're lying face to face with one of her legs slung over your waist and you're thrusting happily but you're not sure it's doing much for her—unfortunately, it might not be. This is similar to the missionary position in that what makes it orgasmic for her, doesn't necessarily make it orgasmic for you. If she moves herself further up your body, so that her knee is under your arm and your penis is firmly inside her, she'll be able to get reasonably good clitoral stimulation from your pubic mound, the area just above your penis. She can also use her leg to push on your buttocks to gain even more pressure at the rhythm she likes on her clitoris.

For you to get good thrusting action, however, you need to be positioned lower down—to give you a decent run up and down her vaginal canal. So the answer is to alternate between the two, or if you want her to climax first, concentrate on being deep inside her and grinding your entire pubic region on hers to give her lip and clitoral stimulation. Then, when she's had hers, get yours through some deep thrusting.

Scissors for great, lazy sex

To give her clitoris more stimulation when you're face to face, twist up your angle a little: if she can flip on to her back, slide one leg between yours, with the other over the top of your hips, keeping you inside her, you're in the scissors position. By holding each other's hands, you can pull your pelvises together and really massage her clitoris and vaginal mound.

Spoons for when she's pregnant

Think about it: when a woman is pregnant there's even more blood rushing down toward her genital area to prepare her body for the birth. All that blood makes her far more responsive to touch, and many women find themselves hungering for sex during the second and third trimesters. But if either of you is worried about how to approach sex while she's pregnant, try the spoons position. By lying down side by side with you behind her, the bump is out of the way but it can be propped up on a pillow so that it's not uncomfortable for her. One hand is free to play with her, by now, fulsome, heavy breasts, and the other can stimulate her clitoris as you thrust inside her. Lots of women report more intense orgasms while pregnant, so take this opportunity to get her saying, "Oh baby!" before the baby comes.

For lazy ladies

I'd put money on the fact that if you offered a woman an orgasm—no effort involved—she'd say yes 99 percent of the time; but if you offer her sex, that percentage would drop dramatically. Why? Because it involves effort! So, for tired women, try the Lazy Susan position: lift her legs so both are bent over your hip, then, lying on your side slide yourself into her vagina. Hold on to her shoulders to give yourself something to thrust against (if she's really tired or lethargic, she'll just shunt up the bed each time you thrust and end up falling off) and don't forget to use your hands to stimulate her clitoris. Use the thumb of whichever hand you're not resting on and rub the heel of your thumb over her clitoris to bring her to orgasm.

Standing

Although it's one of the least-appreciated sex positions of all, don't give standing a wide berth because it's tricky; learn how to make it work.

Staying on your feet

Ask any comedian—stand-up is the most difficult thing to get right. And two people rarely have exactly the right proportions to make it work easily, but don't be fooled into thinking that two tall people find it easier than if one were short; it's not about where your heads meet, it's whether your genitals can connect. And this is one time when being slightly smaller than average can actually benefit a man. Because, if a man's legs are slightly shorter than his partner's, stand-up sex becomes easier because he can thrust upwards without making her topple over. If she's much smaller than you are, you're either going to have to be a big-muscle man and give her a lift, or you can try doing it with her on the stairs to give her a bit more height.

Using props is always a good idea. In the bathroom, forget the shower and make use of the sink. It's one of the most underused sex aids in the house—not only do most sinks have a mirror behind them, giving you both fantastic visuals, but also she can rest her hands on the sink as you do it standing up from behind or front-on with her buttocks on the sink rim.

Note: This is best attempted using sinks with pedestal stands—otherwise your rigorous activity won't make you come; instead, your sink will come away from the wall.

Turn on the cold tap for the occasional breathtaking splash of cold water and this'll turn into a sexual memory to make you grin every time you brush your teeth.

When sex has become routine

Orgasms don't make great sex—if you both come in the same way every time, even climaxing can feel a bit like an anticlimax. Great sex is about exploration, whether that's exploring new aspects of your bodies, new feelings, or new positions. It's difficult to do something new when you've gotten used to doing it well a certain way, but there's no better way to kill a great sex life than to just keep doing it exactly the same way week in, week out. Don't feel you have to swing from the chandeliers or hang upside-down each time you get into bed with each other. But do try to surprise each other with something new every few weeks or so—even if it's just a different way of touching, kissing, or talking.

In my opinion, standing-up sex is one of the most fun ways to reintroduce excitement. It's tricky to get right—especially if you have a big height difference—but it's a position that says lust, passion, and immediacy. That's probably because it's the position new couples go for when they feel they simply haven't got time to get on to the floor or to a bed. That's passion! And the very fact that you can't do it standing up on your bed sets it apart from all the other positions because you have to do it somewhere else in the house or hotel room. OK, it might be against the bedroom wall, but at least you've moved off the bed. When you're used to having sex lying down, doing it standing up changes everything. What you see is different; the weight of your bodies is differently distributed; the blood is even pumped around your body differently. Come on, it's time to stand up and be counted.

Great for discreet, quiet sex

Sometimes having to be quiet and secretive makes sex even more exciting and intense, but if you're staying at the in-laws for longer than just a few days it just becomes an annoyance. Every creak of the bedstead makes you wince and you're unable to relax and really go for it because you can't handle the thought of her parents' faces as you head down for breakfast. The solution? Do it standing up from behind with her hands against a wall. There is always at least one part of a room that doesn't have creaky floorboards, and walls won't make a sound. Now there's no need for you to miss out—call it standing up for your conjugal rights.

Maximizing her pleasure while standing

Of course, I've neglected to point out that stand-up sex rarely results in an orgasm for her. Again, it's tricky to give her clitoris the direct stimulation it needs, but it's not impossible! Slipping your hand under the back of her knee and lifting it up toward her waist and to the side will make this so much easier. Not only does it allow you to control the thrusting rhythm, it also exposes her clitoris and vaginal lips more, giving her far more stimulation. Even better, have her put one foot on a step for the same effect without you having to use your hands, leaving them free to roam all over her fantastic body.

Real Girls Tell All

CARRIE on her favorite position:

"I straddle my man when he's on the sofa watching TV. At first, he moans and pushes me off, says he's watching something. But he laughs, so I know he doesn't really mean it. I just sit on him, moving my pussy around on his penis and balls; he pretends to carry on watching TV but I can feel he's getting stiff underneath me. I think that's half the thrill, knowing I can make him want me even when he's saying he doesn't. Then I unbutton my top or lift my T-shirt and touch my stomach and boobs. By now, he's really hard but he's still pretending to watch TV. Eventually he puts his hands on my hips and helps me gyrate on top of him. That's usually when I come. Then it's his turn."

SUSAN on her favorite position:

"Missionary, missionary, missionary. It just doesn't get better. His face next to mine, kissing me, telling me how much he loves me, how much he wants me, what an amazing orgasm he's going to give me. The feeling of his body weight on top of mine, his shoulders above me so I can hold on when I need to, his legs in between mine. The sense of being totally filled and touched from my face and neck, my arms, hands, fingers, my breasts, nipples, my belly, my legs, my thighs, and of course my vagina. It's the most complete feeling I can ever have and I wouldn't have it any other way."

GILLIAN on her favorite position:

"I once did it on the stairs with a one-night stand and it was just brilliant. He stood in front and below me and I held on to the banister for support, but because of where my feet were I could spread my legs really wide and he penetrated me deeply. It was one of the sexiest experiences I've ever had."

5

Giving oral

Every man thinks he's a master when it comes to his mouth—whether this refers to his apparent storytelling skills down at the pub or going down on a woman. But in reality only the men who know that there's no such thing as "being the best at giving head" can lay legitimate claim to that title—because whereas there are basic rules, each woman will get off on a slightly different technique to the next. And even once you've got it right with the woman you're with, sticking with the same old technique time after time is like giving her a red rose every year for Valentine's Day—nice but lacking imagination. I'll give you ideas that can help make the difference between reaching that climax peak and having to remain in the shadows of the mountain, never quite getting to the top.

Finding Your Way

Knowing your route, how long it'll take and what to look for once you've arrived are essential aspects of a well-executed journey—in this section, we'll address ways to make your oral road to her orgasm a smooth one.

Don't go down too early

Heading down there at high speed is like putting her dessert on the table before you've served appetizers and the main course. She may be looking forward to the dessert more than anything else, but she'll want the savory experience, too—it provides a buildup and makes the end of the meal even sweeter. An orgasm is the release of sexual tension, so the more you build that tension, the greater the eventual release will be.

It's also about intimacy; once your head has disappeared down below and she's left with the sight of your forehead for company, it can be a bit disconcerting, especially if you've only been kissing and touching for a short time. But what constitutes a "short" time? That depends on the woman, but here's an easy way to check if she's ready: if you've been kissing her breasts and nipples and she hasn't been pulling you back up to kiss her lips, start a journey with your hands. Let one hand work its way to her vulva—if she's not ready for clitoral stimulation yet, she'll move away or bring your hand back up. If she lets your hand roam free, gradually work your other hand to take over the work your mouth was doing on her breasts, setting your face free to venture south.

Note: As always, sex rules are there to be broken: 95 percent of the time, waiting until she's fully warmed up before heading down is your best bet, but if you're enjoying the kind of red-hot passion session that causes shirt buttons to fly and stockings to be ripped, then rapidly raising her skirt to feast might be just the thing.

When she's not quite to your taste

This is every woman's nightmare, the thought that she might not smell or taste quite right and so you might not be so enthusiastic when you're down there; worse, you might never go down there again.

To avoid any bad feelings, you need to somehow "taste the waters" before it's too late (worst-case scenario is to go delving with your tongue, then rapidly pull away). If you find her smell or taste unpleasant, there's no point in trying to fake it—if she's in any doubt about your enthusiasm to be down there, she'll be wondering what's wrong, which means she won't orgasm. The result? You'll be stuck down there even longer! So use your fingers down there first, then give them a sniff or a lick when you're kissing her neck so she can't see what you're up to. If it doesn't smell fresh enough for your taste, you have two choices: avoid going down there during this bedroom session or suggest a shower. And if you go for the shower option, make sure you make it about getting sexy rather than getting clean: "Shall we do it in the shower?" rather than "Let's go and wash before we get down to it."

What is a normal smell?

It's important here to differentiate between a woman's natural smell and bad vaginal odor. The former is musky, like a more subtle, warmer, and sweeter version of fresh underarm sweat; the latter is like bad breath, rancid and unnatural smelling. The musky odor has a purpose: scientists believe that one of the reasons we still have hair between our legs and under our arms is to capture and enhance our genetic odor—it's a way of giving each other genetic information without having to chat about our ancestry or medical history. Pubic hair also helps protect the genitals from infection by creating a hairy barrier to liquids that could otherwise be absorbed. But don't be duped into believing that removing the hair will remove any odors; far from it, it might make them worse. Removing her pubes could disrupt the natural pH balance of the vagina and can expose her genitals to bacteria that might otherwise be held at bay.

Getting past her hair and lips

Some women are confident enough to spread their legs wide and let you in; others aren't. If you can't get full access or her lips are getting in your way, put your hands to good use.

Gently slide your hand down her stomach and onto her thigh, easing it away from the other one—this will open up her vaginal lips a little. Now, keep using your hands: place your thumb toward the lower end of her vaginal lips (nearer her anus) where her lips usually sit further apart, and slide your thumb upwards to her belly button, use your other hand to help hold the other lip to one side. This clears the path to her clitoris just like a plow through a field of earth—now follow your thumb with your tongue to find that precious seed at the top of the trough.

Still can't find her clitoris?

If you're licking her all over her lips in an effort to find her pleasure point, don't panic. At this stage she doesn't realize you don't know where it is, she just thinks you're one of the rare (and wonderful) men who spend time exploring and learning about her vulva before heading straight for the clitoris. Some women have huge visible clitorises—the size of a broad bean—others have such tiny ones, you wouldn't bother eating it if it were a pea. But all women have thousands of nerve endings in their vaginal lips as well as that little clitoral button—so explore away, you're getting her well-oiled for the drive of a lifetime.

If you're desperate to get into that driving seat but still can't locate the clitoral gearshift, there is a foolproof way to find it. All women have two outer lips and two inner—they're large and small, fat and thin, never the same and almost never look like the genitals of porn stars who have usually had cosmetic surgery. Start licking at the bottom of her lips, where her vagina is (her vagina isn't the entire genital area, as is often thought, but the "hole" where your penis goes during penetrative sex), and get your tongue between her inner lips. As you slide your tongue from the bottom toward the top—in the direction of her pubic mound or her belly button—you'll reach a point where the lips meet. This is like the corner of your mouth. It's in this area, the "upper corner" of her genital mouth, where you'll find the clitoris.

And if you still can't pinpoint that sexually explosive pea, concentrate your entire tongue on this upper corner—let your tongue flatten against your chin as you grind your face on the entire area. This technique works well for a lot of women because even if the clitoris can't be seen or felt, it's still receiving plenty of stimulation from the pressure your face provides.

When the going gets tough...

Women are, by and large, caring creatures, and so if you've been down there for what feels like forever to you, it's likely she realizes it's taking a while and that'll make her less able to relax...which means she's less likely to come. The problem is that both men and women have the idea that once you're down, you stay down until you've got the job done, but sometimes you just need to take a break—doing so will bring positive results for both of you. Taking a break doesn't mean running downstairs for a cup of coffee, it simply means changing what you're doing. Break off from licking her, and let your fingers do the talking for a few minutes; spend a bit of time kissing her inner thighs or try talking while you're down there. A lot of women find the vibrations from your vocal chords give a fantastic tingling sensation—it's like using a softly spoken vibrator.

Technique

The longest, strongest tongue won't cut the mustard with any woman unless you know how to use it. Rhythm, pressure, speed, variation, and pattern, and all-important saliva, are what you need to be thinking about. And that's what I'll help you do right now.

Easy on the pressure

The clitoris is not a magic button that must be found at all costs and pressed repeatedly until you get her orgasmic bells ringing—the clitoris head is even more sensitive than your penis and some women simply can't handle having it touched directly. It is, however, the key to her orgasm—a woman cannot orgasm without stimulation to her clitoris (scientists believe that even a "vaginal orgasm" occurs through stimulation of the clitoris, but via the "arms" that extend back into her body rather than the head that's visible), but the stimulation needn't be direct. While masturbating, women may use the palm of their hand, a flat vibrator, or even a pillow—this allows for stimulation of the entire area, lips included, without putting too much pressure directly on the clitoris. So how can you simulate that in the bedroom? Easy—use your mouth and chin, and bring your tongue out only for the occasional flat pressure-lick. By using your lips, you can't apply the same zoned pressure on her clitoris as you could with your tongue (try it on your hand and you'll see), but you'll still be providing ample stimulation to the entire region—plenty to bring her to orgasm. Be thankful; pressing your lips into her vulva rather than having to use your tongue on her clitoris will save you a lot of tongue ache. Good news for her, too—that means you'll be able to engage in some post-sex talking.

Practice makes perfect

Keeping up a constant pressure and rhythm is no mean feat—but the tongue, just like any part of the body, can be worked on to become fitter and stronger. Midori, a world-renowned sex teacher, shows her pupils how to perfect oral technique by using fruit as well as a mint candy (you'll have to ask her about that one). She suggests using a plum to strengthen your tongue muscles—you simply keep licking and applying pressure until the skin breaks. Then once you've broken through, you've got to find your way to the plum's stone and get it out! Do that regularly and your muscles will grow to be big and strong.

And, just as you would after eating a plum, lick your lips after going down on a woman, don't wipe. That's the gentlemanly—and very sexy—thing to do.

Forget about licking the alphabet

This old trick has been written about in several sex books and magazines, but I'm yet to meet a woman who says it'll bring her to orgasm. There is a small possibility that she'll climax by having the alphabet licked onto her clitoris, but chances are it will be interesting, exciting even, for no more than a half a minute or so—as a teaser—quite quickly it will feel rather frustrating, like being in bed with a man who has to change sex position after every thrust. Keep the alphabet trick for times you'd like to play with her or get her aroused, but don't rely on it to bring her to orgasm, as you're unlikely to succeed.

Use your hands, too

Ever enjoyed a woman's hands squeezing your behind while giving you oral? Ever reached climax as she's played with your nipples while sucking you? Ever been sent over the edge as she's handled your balls while going down? Well, what a coincidence—women also like to be touched when a man goes down on them. Trouble is, most men (and women when the roles are reversed) are so focused on the task in hand—their tongue and lips and her lips and clitoris—that they forget she even has a body with plenty of other erogenous zones that will bring her to a more explosive orgasm sooner.

Try any of these hands-on approaches:

- **Start at the bottom.** Grab her behind to give yourself better access and extra stimulation power—you can push up as you lick down, maximizing the effects of your tongue or lips.

- **Find her breasts.** If you have long enough arms to play with her love pillows at the same time as giving her oral, you'll be rewarded with plenty of brownie points.

- **Press on her pubic mons.** That's the bony pubic area above her vagina. Don't do it hard, but if you pull the flesh back here you expose her clitoris and many women really enjoy the sensation.

- **Don't forget her hands.** Grabbing her hands is a nice intimate thing to do when you're giving her oral, plus it also gives you extra control—you can pull her body down onto your face if you have both of her hands in yours.

Techniques to bring her to orgasm quicker

Use one of the following moves when you go down on her, but don't forget to experiment: try variations of each and make up new techniques!

The no-move move

Simply hold your tongue firm and let her do the moving and shaking. As sex therapist Dr. Ian Kerner puts it, "A flat, still tongue is one of the most underestimated oral-sex techniques." And he's so right. If women most enjoyed flicking, darting tongues, they'd invest in a lizard—have you ever even seen a sex toy designed to look like one? No. That's because they prefer a firm, even pressure. Hold your tongue and you'll hold the key to her orgasm.

The tip massage

Using the tip of your tongue, run it from above her clitoris (near her pubic mound) to the clitoris head itself—you should be able to feel a thin elastic "thread" running along this line, this is the equivalent of your penis's frenulum (or banjo string). Now hook your tongue under the clitoris head and, pushing down, bring your tongue back up again. Her clitoris has a "hood" just like the foreskin on your penis, that can be pushed and pulled down and up—that's what you're doing with this move.

The cow-lick

Using your thumbs to keep her lips apart, use the flat, middle part of your tongue on her clitoris. Rather than moving your tongue, repeatedly move your head and shoulders up and down an inch or so. She will inevitably begin to gyrate her hips in time with your movements or in a different rhythm. If she goes for the different option, just hold your head still and let her do the work.

The roundhouse lick

Like the legendary roundhouse kick by Patrick Swayze in the film *Road House*, this involves using a full range of motions. Because the clitoris has two "arms" that extend back into the vaginal lips (in terms of size, it's actually bigger than the penis), you can bring a woman closer to orgasm if you stimulate her lips as well as her clitoris. With this move, lick in between her inner and outer lips from the bottom to the top and back down again on the other side; repeat until you feel dizzy, then do it anticlockwise. For many women, this will bring them to orgasm more easily because of the extra stimulation to their lips. But if your woman needs more direct clitoral action, gradually reduce the area you're covering with your tongue, until you're just rubbing her clitoris.

The dribble

This isn't actually a move, it's a rule to live by when going down on your woman—licking her with a dry mouth is like kissing without lips: practically pointless. Have a sip of water, suck on a mint, or chew gum—the latter will keep your breath fresh, give you more saliva, and give her a tingling minty sensation down below.

Sometimes you need to keep a straight face

If she's gyrating her hips like mad and you're desperately trying to keep up, stop—just keep your head still! Sometimes you're so, so close to bringing her to that sweet moment of orgasmic release, but because you're not totally in tune with her body, you're not quite getting there. If she's gyrating in a certain way, keep doing whatever it is you were doing—or simply stop. By trying to change what you're doing to adapt to her moves, you may be doing the opposite of what she needs. If you're using an up and down motion and she's circling her hips, for example, it may simply mean that she needs both those actions to hit the mark. Sometimes it's easiest to keep your face in the same place and let her show you the kind of pressure and rhythm she really likes. Be glad—this way you'll know exactly what does the trick for next time.

Keep the pace

Increasing speed may be the key to greater success in the world of Formula One racing, but it's not what will get you to the finishing line in the run up to her orgasm. Generally speaking, if she's enjoying what you're doing, don't change a thing—just keep the same pace, the same movement, the same rhythm and she'll get to orgasm sooner than if you change anything. Men who suffer from premature ejaculation are often told to change sex position regularly to avoid climax, the idea being that by changing the stimulus the body has to readapt. And in a sense, increasing the speed or changing the pressure when you're going down on a woman amounts to the same thing: by doing so, you prevent her from climbing the climax ladder. Hold it steady instead, and she'll get up and over the top far sooner.

When she's about to come

Sometimes a woman is so close, so tantalizingly close to orgasm that she daren't move lest you stop what you're doing or she loses the "moment" and then doesn't get there. In an ideal world, she'll give you some idea of this by gasping out a, "Yes!" or "I'm going to come" while you're down there, but chances are, if she's really close, she won't be able to utter a word. So how can you tell? Her body will be tense; it won't be floppy or relaxed. Keep a hand on her inner thigh or stomach to judge this—if you can feel her stomach muscles tense, she's not asleep—she's probably just in a position where she's getting maximum pleasure and wants you to keep going.

Women often shudder and jerk after they've had a particularly powerful orgasm, but she'll let you know if she's had enough—quite possibly by sliding up the bed away from your head, closing her legs or, if she's a classy lady, putting her hand on your face to pull it up toward hers and giving you a kiss to say thank you for giving her such a great time.

She doesn't want oral!

There are lots of reasons why she may not enjoy it: it might make her feel uncomfortable for emotional reasons; she might be insecure about the way she looks or smells; or you might just need more practice (in which case, keep reading). But it may also be that she simply enjoys the sensation of having a penis inside her—for some women, penetration is a sexy feeling and they want that for orgasm. If that's the problem, you can easily solve it with your fingers, a dildo, or a vibrator.

If you're using your fingers, you may find it difficult to get your head and your hand into position. One method to try, if she's lying on her back, is to use the thumb of your left hand inside her vagina, propping yourself up with your right arm. Alternatively, you can kneel on her right-hand side, lean on your right elbow between her legs and use the same hand's fingers to penetrate her, leaving your other hand free to touch her breasts or stimulate her vaginal lips while you lick. A dildo or vibrator makes the task easier, and with a vibrator you have the added advantage of the vibrations, of course.

Don't stick with what works

Even when something works perfectly, it's still fun to stir it up every now and again. Try using your nose instead of your mouth and tongue. It might sound odd, but when you think about it, the nose is perfectly designed to be a clitoral stimulator—it's firmer than a tongue but with enough give not to be too hard like a finger can be; it's not a muscle so it won't get tired; and it leaves you free to breathe through your mouth. She may not even realize you're using your nose, but she's sure to appreciate the sensation.

Another thing to try is a vibrator. Hold it against your jawbone as you go down on her and it'll carry the vibrations to the rest of your mouth. Or try humming (warn her you're going to try this before you do it, otherwise she'll be worried for your sanity); this produces vibrations, too.

And there's always food: but forget your standard strawberries and cream; although delicious they don't provide much extra sensation. To really experiment with different sensations down there, use food with different temperatures. Mango, halved and with its skin still on, lightly warmed in an oven, feels fantastic mashed up against the entire vulva; and if you must do it with strawberries, cut them in half and put them in the freezer for 40 minutes—that's just enough to get them nice and cold, perfect for creating a nice cold sensation to contrast with the warmth of your tongue.

Best Positions

Oral sex misses out when it comes to positions—all the focus is on penetrative sex and the different variations you can try. This section should change that, because oral is all about the angle.

On your knees

This position is great for men who suffer from neck- or backache and women who like complete stimulation.

By positioning yourself on your knees on the floor at the foot of the bed, with her body on the bed and her feet on the floor on either side of you, your back is in a far more natural position than if you're crouched in between her legs on the bed. Your neck can remain straight instead of being bent crooked, which will make the entire experience more comfortable and enjoyable. This also works really well on the stairs.

This position allows far greater access to her lips and clitoris, too—you can let your head and tongue go as low as you like without the bed getting in the way. The area between a woman's vagina and anus, the perineum, is highly sensitive to touch—use this to your advantage and lick her in places she didn't know she loved to be licked.

On her knees

This is great for men who want to have an easy life and women who know exactly how to bring themselves to orgasm.

Putting a few plump pillows behind your head and shoulders, she kneels on all fours facing your feet—her buttocks facing your face. Arching her back allows you access and if you trust her not to suffocate you with her fleshy peaches, she can control the movements by thrusting with her body on and off or around your tongue and face. Your hands are free to play with her breasts (it's easiest to slide your arm in between her legs) or her derrière, or you can place a strategic finger inside her vagina and put pressure on her G-spot, about 5cm (2in) up inside her vagina's front wall.

Her on her side

Try it with her on her side and your head in between her thighs: great for men who like a headrest and women who like anal stimulation.

This is not the classic 69 position, where your bodies are top to tail. Instead, your head is in between her legs but you are facing her (so the rest of your body is below and behind her body). You can easily rest your head on her thigh and she can rest her upper leg on your shoulder so that she doesn't crush your head in a vice-like orgasmic grip. Your hands are free to stimulate her from behind, if she so wishes.

69

This is great for men and women who can multitask.

The much-lauded 69 position is without doubt one of the most difficult to master. Concentrating on bringing a man or woman to orgasm through oral sex is a job enough in itself, without having to relax and enjoy the sensation of great oral sex on yourself. It's a lot like patting the top of your head and rubbing your stomach in circular motions—you can get it right for a bit, but eventually one or the other motion takes over. In the 69 position that tends to mean that one or other partner stops focusing on the task in hand—the other person's orgasm.

And it's not just about finding it difficult to enjoy giving and receiving pleasure simultaneously, it's also about practicality: some people simply aren't physically matched for 69. A very tall man and a small woman, for example, will find that just as her mouth reaches the tip of his penis her vulva is pulled just out of reach of his searching tongue.

For all its difficulties, however, it's a lot of fun trying. Try it with one partner on all fours above the other, top to tail. Whoever is on top has far more control of what's going on, which can prove frustrating to the "under person,' but at least this way one rhythm and pace is kept to, making it easier. You can also try it lying on your sides—that is, facing each other, top to tail. This relaxed approach means that you can kiss, lick, and suck each other and use your hands, too.

Standing

This is great for men who love to give and women who love to dominate.

Not only will standing, rather than lying down, give her an entirely different orgasmic experience, but this is also a fantastic position for showing just how much you lust for her. To have a man go down on one knee is one thing, but to have him go down on both knees and lick like a puppy-dog is a pleasure every woman should enjoy.

Real Girls Tell All

NICKY on her first oral experience:

"I had no idea what he was doing—I didn't even know it was something people did—but I didn't stop him. I still had my panties on and he was just breathing on me, cupping his hands around his mouth so his breath was concentrated in just that one small area. It was like he breathed life into my sexuality. That sounds a bit over the top but it really was like that—it was the first time anyone had even touched me down there and I was instantly excited, but I didn't even really know what that feeling was. The feeling spread from in between my legs to up my stomach and down my legs, and over my whole body—all he was doing was breathing but it felt so, so good. I'd love for someone to just breathe on me like that again; it was one of the most amazing experiences of my life."

EMILY on her fantasy oral experience:

"I've never had really great oral sex, but when I fantasize I imagine a man with a really thick tongue. It's no ordinary tongue! He licks me all over with his tongue, then he gets down in between my legs and he licks my thighs hard, he licks everywhere hard—but he hasn't got a pointed tongue, it's almost flat at the tip, like a hammer-head shark's head! That's why it's so good—it's almost like having two tongues at once because it's wide and thick. He pushes up and down my lips, not touching my clit, because he knows how to get me going. Then, at the same time as I let myself touch my clit (I've been fingering around my lips while I've been thinking all this), he puts his tongue on my clit. He pushes down on it and pulls back up, and he's enjoying it so much that it's like he's going to come, too, just from doing it to me. That's it. That's my fantasy. Does it for me every time!"

JOANNA on her boyfriend's technique:

"He's just amazing. He eats me like I'm the tastiest steak he's ever seen and he's been starved for months. Honestly, it's like he really wants to eat me. He uses his whole mouth, not just his tongue like some guys do. His lips squeeze on my lips; he pushes with his lips and sucks on my lips, too. I don't let him bite, that just hurts. He talks while he's down there, too. He says how much he wants to eat me, how much he loves me, and how good I taste—it makes me giggle but it turns me on so much, too. It's like he really does love going down on me, like it really gives him as much pleasure as it does me. When I've come, he sits up with a big satisfied grin on his face—just like he would if he'd had a good meal. I love that man."

6

Getting oral

You may wonder what fellatio has to do with blowing a woman's mind in bed—after all, it's all about you, right? Wrong. Women, just like men, enjoy sex more if they believe they've given their partner a fantastic experience. We want to be the best you've ever had, and many women are extremely proud of their blow-job abilities ...and not always justifiably, as I found out when talking to a male colleague of mine: "When it comes to talking about fellatio skills, women love to blow their own trumpets. But most women I've met can't blow a penis properly, let alone a trumpet," he told me. And according to one poll on a men's website, the majority of men would probably agree with him—as six out of ten men said they had never achieved an orgasm during fellatio. Not a high success rate!

But I think there's more to this than women's apparent inability to bring a man to orgasm with their mouths. Women tend to use oral sex as a preamble to penetrative sex in much the same way as men do with cunnilingus—they don't see it as a worthy end in its own right. Adjusting her attitude toward it is key to making the experience better for her and for you.

First Times

Even the most experienced, confident woman will be uncertain of how successful she'll be when she goes down on you. No two men are the same in the technique they enjoy and each penis is unique, too.

She's got big, juicy blow-job lips

If you're thinking her mouth was made for blow jobs, chances are every other man she's ever met or been with has thought the same. Don't join the predictables by expecting, or worse, suggesting she gives you head with those BJ lips of hers. Instead, keep showing her you're committed to her pleasure by giving her plenty of oral sex. Women are more naturally inclined to be givers rather than receivers—but when the gift, in this case oral sex, is expected, it takes all the pleasure out of giving. It's not dissimilar to when you've already picked something out for her birthday, for example; something you know she wants, but she can't help dropping enormous hints to let you know she wants it. Where's the pleasure in being told how to be giving?

A man who expects or demands fellatio is a man who'll end up with a partner who resents it. Women with BJ lips are even more likely to feel like this, as it's highly likely that men have impressed upon them how great their lips are for the task. It's also a lot to live up to—big lips do not a good blow job make. Far from it; the size of her lips is largely irrelevant. Unless she knows how to use them, and we'll come to that later, oral sex can be wholly unsatisfactory or mind-blowingly good.

Making sure you taste good

You'd be amazed at how just one little drop of your golden pee can infuse your entire genital region with eau de urine. Some of the most hygienic, clean-living, nice-smelling men have odorous genitals. I blame a lack of toilet-tissue use. The majority of men prefer to shake their tails, then place them back inside their underpants, despite the fact that droplets undoubtedly remain. If you've ever tried shaking water out of a wine glass, for example, you'll see how impossible it is to shake water off an object—and a wine glass is smooth and shiny, so even easier to shake liquid off. Your penis is skin and so holds liquid on it, absorbs it even. Use tissue to dab away at your end and not only will your genital area smell sweeter but also you won't come out of the toilet with splash marks on your trousers.

And if you want her to get down there and be really enthusiastic, wash thoroughly first. If you use soap and water, you must rinse thoroughly—soapy mouth is as bad as pee-underpants. So have a shower, use a bidet or just use plain water to give her the best fellatio experience possible.

The taste of your semen

Some women love it, some hate it, but most find it not exactly pleasant but not disgusting either. Personally, I think it's a bit like watery, slightly salted semolina—not the best thing I've ever tasted, but certainly not the worst (the durian fruit in Thailand, if you must know—smells and tastes like rotten flesh). To make yours taste better, avoid strongly flavored foods. If you've ever noticed how your body odor changes after you've been eating garlic or onion, or drinking alcohol or coffee, that's the same kind of flavor she'll get in your semen. Semen is made up of water, small amounts of salt, fructose sugar, and protein—these "ingredients" all come from your body, so they're bound to take on a mild version of the flavor of whatever you've been eating. Try drinking lots of water, and eating plenty of fruit to sweeten it. Your armpits will smell better, too. Bonus!

But don't get too hung up on the flavor, as often it's the texture of your ejaculate that's off-putting. If you get lumps in your semen, it could be a build up of old semen mixing with new—so the answer is to masturbate. It's good for you—see "Hands-Solo Style," pages 166-170, on masturbation to find out more reasons why.

When she's too quick to head down there

Ever had a woman head down there after just a few minutes of kissing? You may have loved it, but chances are, you're a little freaked by her eagerness—you may not be ready to have her down there.

The problem lies in how we perceive oral sex. There's a myth that most women subscribe to, and that's that men love blow jobs above all else—above penetrative sex, above beer, above sports, even. Ask most men if this is the case and they'll say they enjoy penetrative sex more, and some will even say fellatio is hugely overrated. But in many women's minds, it's the ultimate sexual gift. Why? The media and porn films undoubtedly contribute to its popularity, but I think schools and parents also help give fellatio a special status. Teenagers are taught about procreation and penetrative sex; their parents may even tell them how it all works, but will they describe fellatio, too? It's less likely. And so teenage boys become obsessed with knowing what it is, giggling about it and writing about it on toilet walls. Without realizing it, they're sending a message to a generation of young women that says, "We love blow jobs more than anything else."

If it feels too soon for her to be heading down there, gently take her head up toward yours and kiss her. I hear from more and more men who complain that too many women just want to take things too fast. Don't let her set the pace if it's too soon for you; it'll only ruin it for both of you in the long run. If she needs an explanation as to why you didn't want to let her fellate you, just tell her you were getting really turned on kissing her. She'll be surprised, but she won't be disappointed.

Slowing the blowing

Lots of women head between a man's legs, then go at it like a bobbing woodpecker—they mistakenly believe that this is the easiest and quickest way to bring you to orgasm. Men are always being told to slow down, to let women get in the mood—I've probably said it several times in this book—but women are rarely told to take it down a couple of gears, because there's an assumption that men are always ready. But men, just like women, will get far more aroused and have stronger and stiffer erections, and more powerful orgasms, if they are teased, flirted, played with, and seduced. But because lots of our sexual "knowledge" comes from pornography or television erotica, where men are ready to go—go at it hard—ejaculating copious amounts of semen everywhere, we think all men like it hard and fast all the time.

Then there's the other problem: that blow jobs are often something women would quite frankly like to get over and done with, with as little fuss and effort as possible. That's not always the case, and some women absolutely love giving head, but even when you love it, it's hard work! Imagine spending more than five minutes sucking a washed zucchini (deep throat too!) and tell me how you think your mouth and jaw would feel. Holding your mouth around something for a long period of time is effort in itself, but add to that the need to apply pressure, swirl your tongue around, use your hands, and possibly throw in some moaning to add to the experience, and it's a real task. No wonder women are paid to do it—and why it's called a blow job.

So how can you make her slow down or ease up if you want to? Use your hands and your mouth—place a hand on the underside of her jaw as though you're cupping her face to kiss her; that is, don't grab—that will help slow her head movements down, and as you do so, moan or breathe deeply and slowly. Women are used to using non verbal communication to read people and so changing your breath or moaning like this should help give her an indicator to slow down. Using your hand emphasizes the rhythm you're hoping for and she should slow down. This is also a good technique for suggesting she goes faster later on.

Those teeth, those teeth!

Blame Jackie Collins—I do. Reading her books as a young teenager gave me much of the knowledge of fellatio and sex I took with me into my first sexual experiences. And in her books, good sex always comes with power, money, and a little bit of pain—the exciting sexy female character would take her man into her mouth and let her teeth sink into his skin, making him scream in pleasure. But it's not just Jackie Collins; read a few sex advice books and there's often a mention of dragging teeth along the penis to heighten sensation or to spice things up a bit.

And, of course, some men do get off on the feeling, but not many (some men also enjoy having their testicles rubbed with a cheese grater, but it's certainly not the norm). If the two people in a couple trust each other, playing with pain-pleasure can make things exciting—the uncertainly of how hard she'll bite or the near-pain of her dragging teeth could make the sex seem more passionate, more out of control. But if you don't know each other well enough for that level of trust, or if it really doesn't do it for you, as is the case for most men, you need to get her to stop—fast.

Luckily, there's an easy and quick solution to this: saying "Ow!" once is enough to stop her ever trying the teeth-dragging experiment again. Yes, it's harsh, but once said, the problem is solved.

No skin versus foreskin

It's not just women who get confused about what to do with a circumcised penis if they're used to a non-circumcised one and vice versa—even men do. I've had readers asking me how to masturbate because they've just been circumcised.

If she's only known circumcised guys...
A woman who's only known circumcised penises will firstly be amazed at all this "excess" skin and what to

do with it. But more importantly, she'll also likely be scared of hurting you if you haven't been cut. It's that frenulum, or banjo string as it's often called, attaching your foreskin to your penis. It looks like it could snap, just like a real banjo string, and so she imagines that yanking about on your penis, your foreskin, is kind of dangerous.

If she's touching you like you're a piece of Ming Dynasty china, it's time to take her in hand. Place your hand over hers and apply pressure so she can see how she can manipulate you without causing pain. She'll soon get the hang of it, and eventually she'll find it just as easy as she did with circumcised guys.

If she's only known uncircumcised guys ...
For this woman, the cut guy presents somewhat of a conundrum—she knows that the foreskin can be pulled back and forth to stimulate the penis, so what does she do with this penis without a foreskin? It can be flummoxing, to say the least. Not used to stimulating a penis so directly—that is, being able to touch the entire shaft under the foreskin—can also make her want to be more careful when handling your manhood. Or conversely, it can mean she grabs and uses pressure on your shaft that is actually too painful to bear when it doesn't have a long foreskin to protect

it. Either way, you need to use your hands to show her what to do. And the key to making it work (this goes for masturbating on your own, too) is lubrication: this gives you or her the ability to slide up and down your shaft without too much friction, just enough to bring you to orgasm.

She just won't go down

Some women just don't like the sensation of a penis inside their mouth; others don't like the taste of your skin; and others may dislike the notion of having a man's genitals in their mouth for moral or hygiene reasons. There is absolutely nothing you can do to change a woman's mind if she doesn't like doing it. If she knows it's something that disgusts her, for whatever reason, no matter how hard you plead, she's still going to find it disgusting. All you'll succeed in doing is making her do something she hates, and she'll end up resenting you for it. Never push a woman into going down on you—you'll only end up being pushed out of her bed and her life.

Helping Her to Get It Right

No woman is going to take too kindly to being told she's no good at oral sex, but there's no reason why you can't show her how to get her technique right to make it work for you.

She sucks it like a soft ice cream

Lick it like a lollipop, swirl your tongue around it like an ice cream, and suck on it like a banana—all these bits of fellatio advice are good but they might result in the wrong kind of blow job for you. Women read sex advice in books or magazines, or they talk to their friends, just like you do. The impression given by many friends, magazines, or books is that just one lick of her tongue on your supersensitive, highly charged penis is enough to make it explode in milkiness all over her face. In reality, of course, most men need a bit more stimulation than a quick flick of the tongue.

The best way to encourage her to apply more pressure is to use your mouth. Tell her you want more pressure by saying, "Mmm, you're teasing me." She'll realize that she has to up the pressure and speed in order to stop "teasing" you and to begin seriously pleasuring you. Saying, "Harder!" or "Faster!" is more direct, but sounds like a command. Whereas she might enjoy that, she's more likely to find it irritating and give you your marching orders instead.

She gags whenever she tries to go deep

Why do men enjoy deep throat so much? Because the head of the penis gets stimulated by touching the back of a woman's throat—but it's precisely this touching that usually gives a woman a gag reflex. The very worst thing you can do here is to put your hand on her head and try to guide her or to thrust. In fact, thrusting during fellatio is usually a sure fire way to make sure she gags, as she has no way of controlling how deep down her throat you go. Just let her find her rhythm; let her find the right speed and the depth she can handle.

A position to make it easier

You can also try different angles to help her get more of you inside her. Side-on, if you're lying down, is easier, but the side of her head should be parallel to your belly to make sure your penis goes down her throat rather than into her molars (ouch!). It's often recommended women lie face up on bed with their heads hanging over the edge of a bed to extend and lengthen the throat, while the man penetrates standing up beside her, but this is risky, as the man has to control the thrusting—which, if she's prone to gagging, is likely to make her gag even more. By far the best position is if you're standing by the side of the bed and she is kneeling on it, taking you slightly from one side. This way, you can see what she's doing and she gets complete control and can easily use her hands, too—on your shaft, your buttocks or anywhere else.

She goes at it like she's a vacuum cleaner?

Does she seem desperate to get the job done? Going at it as fast and hard as possible? Yet another myth that needs to be busted: men are not robots who will come when a certain oral sex technique is applied. Men, just like women, enjoy different rhythms, techniques, and speeds when it comes to oral sex. The trouble is, women have been led to believe that a mouth around a man's penis, a hammer up-and-down action, and a few strategic moans are enough to make any man come. The truth is that, just like a man needs to get to know a body anew each time he's with a different woman, understanding how she likes to be touched, kissed, and stimulated, so a woman needs to with a man.

To encourage her to change pace or rhythm, try having sex 69-style, with you on top and her beneath you. That way, you can control the speed with which your penis goes in and out of her mouth but she's also getting something out of the deal. It's a great way for both of you to show each other exactly what style of oral you like. And hopefully you can kiss Woody Woodpecker good-bye.

Stopping and starting: why she does it

A common complaint from men is that women stop and start when giving head, and usually just as they're starting to build up to climax. Poor you. The trouble is that it's an art form getting your breathing right while fellating. And you can forget it if she's got a blocked nose.

You need to encourage her to keep using her hand on your head and shaft at the same rhythm whenever she stops to take her mouth away from your penis. And the best way to keep her doing this is to show her with your own hand, taking over where she's left off, or by giving her signs of how close you are to climax with your breathing and your voice. You'll be amazed at the effect you can have with just the occasional "mmm" or "yeah'—it's often enough to encourage another five full minutes of enthusiastic blow jobbing from her.

Getting more for your oral

We're all guilty of thinking a tongue and lips are enough to bring the opposite sex to orgasm—men think it's enough for cunnilingus, and women do for fellatio, too. But both are dramatically improved with a bit of hands-on action. Take her hand and, with yours on top, show her how she can use it along with her mouth.

Encouraging More Oral

For some men, there is no such thing as too much fellatio—in fact, fellatio is often used as foreplay rather than an end in itself. Kind of unfair, when you consider that so many men are expected to go down on a woman until she orgasms. I believe there are two common themes for women who don't like to go down: they don't like the idea/taste/sensation of you in their mouth, or they're not confident about what they're doing. It's difficult to do much about the first, but the second can be dealt with.

When she gives up too soon

Men's penises are perceived by women, and portrayed by the media, as loaded guns, ready to go off at the slightest touch, and so women are understandably dismayed when they discover that it takes a little more effort than a spot of licking and sucking to get the big explosion. The result is that they think they're no good at it. But as I mentioned earlier, only four out of ten men have ever experienced an orgasm through oral sex. If she knew that, she would undoubtedly feel more confident about going down on you.

To get her to continue and to make her realize she's perfectly capable of taking you to climax, you need to communicate with her while she's down there. You may want to lie back and just enjoy the experience, but unless you give her some guiding "mmm's," "Yes," "That's great," "Don't stop," she won't know that you're getting close to climax nor that you want her to continue. You've got to communicate if you want to get what you want in bed. Men are too reticent in being vocal about what feels good in bed, but if you hold back with the encouragement, the person who loses out is you, because your partners won't know what feels good.

It's always a prelude to penetration

Think about it: once she's made you come, she knows you're going to be pretty useless at continuing sex. Women are expected to be able to continue with sex after they've had an orgasm through oral sex or being stimulated manually; men, however, aren't. It's generally seen as gentlemanly to allow a woman to orgasm first, then it's the man's turn—but that rule only serves to support the idea that once a man's come, the sex is over. Orgasms release sleep-inducing chemicals in both sexes—that's why both men and women masturbate to try get to sleep when it's difficult (yes, women do it, too). And that's also why most people—male or female—would quite happily drift off or relax after they've climaxed.

The trick to changing this situation is changing your attitudes toward sex. Give her an orgasm without having one yourself. Do it several times over a few weeks so that she begins to realize it wasn't a one-off. That way, you introduce the idea that it's not essential for both of you to orgasm each time you get into bed with each other. Then, if there are times in your relationship when one of you is too stressed/disinterested/lazy to orgasm, the other person can enjoy their climax without feeling guilty.

The "you used to give me blow jobs" sob story

She thinks she's impressed you with her bedroom moves, so now she can head into the comfort zone—there's no need for deep-throating any more! It's a common story and it holds true for both sexes—it's all too easy to get lazy.

And as I mentioned earlier, blow jobs are hard work. That said, she shouldn't give up on giving them just because you've been together for a while. Good sexual relationships stay that way because both partners "work" at keeping it good. But don't complain; that will just get her back up. Instead, focus on complimenting her on her skills. When you're having dinner, look wistfully into the distance, with a secret smile on your face. Don't say a word. Give it about 45-60 seconds and she's bound to ask, "What are you thinking about?" Now's your chance: "I was just remembering that time when you..." and describe a time when she gave you a fantastic oral experience. The flattery will get her thinking and it's a nice subtle way to encourage her to do it again.

She knows she's no good

And you know it, too. When she goes down on you, it does nothing for you and she picks up on that—you think it feels nice, but not amazing. What to do? Communicate. Talk. Speak. Show. Tell. Chat. Converse. Just tell her what feels good! How can she improve if you don't talk to her? Try: "What I'd love is if you could squeeze your cheeks in tight when you suck on my penis," "I love it when you press hard with your tongue," or "I wish you'd massage my buttocks as you suck me." Obviously change the words to suit your own preferences.

If saying what you want out loud is too difficult, try reading a book (like this one!) that gives tips and advice for both partners; an instructional sex DVD is even better, as you can see what's going on—and usually, these are designed for couples, so you could say it was for both of you to improve technique and try new things.

More ways to get more

Try introducing new things to the bedroom to encourage oral sex, too. A tongue vibrator is a nice way to introduce new sensations into the experience—an ideal way to encourage her to enjoy it, and it makes it more likely that you'll orgasm, too. And you can use food to make the experience seem more like fun, rather than about her fellatio technique or getting you to orgasm. Try using frozen fruits—if she holds a mouthful of frozen raspberries in her mouth as she licks and sucks you, it draws attention away from her technique and makes it more fun. The cold of the ice and the warmth of her mouth will feel great for you, and fellatio will never have tasted so good for her.

And if all else fails, suggest she reads this for some ideas:

- Starting with a soft penis, take your man in your mouth and suck him as though he were a big lollipop, squeezing with your tongue and your mouth to get the sweet juicy flavor out of it. Don't be too gentle; your tongue and mouth are quite soft anyhow.

- Now that he's hard, play with his penis head. Swallow it with your mouth—cover your teeth with your lips if you have to—and suck your cheeks in so that you create suction on the tip of his penis. Use your tongue to push and explore as you do this.

- Let your lips leave his penis head, but leave your tongue circling it. Focus on the ridge and on the frenulum, if he has one (the piece of skin that connects his foreskin to his penis). Let your tongue ride up and down his shaft. If your mouth is dry, drink some water. Lubrication makes blow jobs so much better.

- "Eat" your way up and down his shaft—use your lips to pull and push on his skin as though you were trying to eat it without your teeth. Keep your tongue moving up and down, too.

- As you do this, use your hands to touch the head of his penis—rub the palm of your hand on the top and use your fingers to give it a gentle squeeze.

- Use your hands elsewhere—on his testicles, on his buttocks, or on his nipples. Now circle your thumb and forefinger around his penis and place your mouth above that circle. Moving them in unison up and down his penis, keep your tongue applying pressure to his penis, but use your hand to apply a firm up-and-down movement. This gives him the delicious sensation of your mouth but the pressure he needs from your hand.

• Twist your hand as you move down ever so slightly to increase the stimulation, release the pressure on the upstroke, then apply it more firmly on the downward stroke. Use both hands as well as your lips and your tongue. Use the rest of your body, too—press your breasts into his leg or on to his hands; use your vocal chords to make noises he'll feel as vibrations on his penis.

• To bring him to climax, listen to his breathing and what he says as you change and try different touches and techniques—when his breathing becomes faster and harder (not necessarily louder), he's getting close to climax. Do not stop whatever it is you're doing. Hold on tight because this rocket's about to lift off!

Real Girls Tell All

SHARON describes how she gives head:

"I've got quite big teeth so I have to fold my lips over the edges when I go down on my man, but I think that actually makes it work even better, because I've got a lot of pressure as I go up and down his shaft. I usually start by licking his shaft from the bottom all the way to the top, flicking my tongue at the top—I'll do that over and over until he's really hard, then I'll give his head a good suck. I make a lot of noise but I think he quite likes that. Then I build up the pressure and eventually I'm really going at it hard; I even break out in a sweat! Right at the end, when I can feel he's going to come, I slow right down—he still comes but he says the orgasm's even better because I don't let it come straight off."

ADIE describes her best fellatio techniques:

"Eye contact, it's all about eye contact. My husband loves it when I look him right in the eye while I'm sucking him off. That's why I always make sure my man is sitting down before I go down on him. I like to unzip him too, and take him out of his underpants—for him and me; it's all part of the process. There's something so sexy about it if he keeps his clothes on. I make sure I lick every last drop of him up, put him back inside, and zip him up. He can't do enough for me for weeks after!"

7

Using your hands on her body

Love may be blind, but we're all feeling in the dark when it comes to sex—mainly because most of us shut or half-close our eyes. And that's what makes your hands so important during sex—with them you're "looking" at her body; you're admiring her breasts or her shapely buttocks or the silky smoothness of her inner thigh. No wonder, then, that in surveys 18 percent of women say hands are the part of your body they're most attracted to. What you do with yours, where you put them, how you move them, and the pressure you use affects far more than your own sense of her body; however, it can be the thing to bring her to orgasm. And you can also help her use her hands to make your sex experience better— because sex isn't all about her; good sex is good for both of you.

Her Body

Make her feel like a goddess by adoring every part of her, but focus on her hot spots, too—these are the places that are most likely to arouse her.

Around her face

You'd be surprised at how much stress she's holding in that pretty face of hers. By giving her temples and forehead a massage, you'll relax her after a hard day—and she'll become aroused only once she's relaxed, so this is a good move to try on any day of the week. And look for her lips to part. If she's uptight or tense her lips will stay shut; when she's feeling more relaxed, they'll fall slightly apart.

On her lips

You'll often touch her lips with yours but don't forget to use your fingers, too. Try touching her lips lightly with your thumb, looking directly at her mouth as you do so, then kissing her. It's a very sexy move.

On the back of her neck

This is a "melt" location. The skin tends to be thinner where the body bends or flexes—backs of the knees, neck, inner elbows, and so on—which means that blood vessels are closer to the skin's surface, making it supersensitive. Moving her hair gently away from her neck to kiss it, or letting your fingers move over her neck, makes her feel exposed, in a good way—it's one of the most sensuous moves you can use.

On her hips

Placing your hands on her hips during a kiss or sex makes her feel feminine and sexy. When you're facing her, try placing your hands low on her hips but letting your thumbs move inwards closer to her pubic area. This is a highly sensitive part of her body because, like on the neck, the blood is very close the surface. Press gently with your thumbs and slide them up and down. Careful, though, this is a hot zone—she might just melt on the spot.

On her behind

Putting your hands on her behind during a kiss makes your intentions clear—if you pull her body in toward yours, pressing her pelvis into yours, it can be a huge turn-on.

On the small of her back

One strategically placed hand on the small of her back to pull her in toward you during a kiss is fantastically romantic and passionate. Like the bum move, it also pulls her pelvis to yours and puts you in control, but this is a little more gentlemanly and the sexier for it. It's also where most of the nerve endings on her back are located—the upper area isn't anywhere near as sensitive.

On her breasts

It goes without saying that her breasts are a fantastic place to touch her if you want to get her aroused or give her pleasure. Since they're packed with nerve endings, you don't need to be rough to get a good response: feather-light touching will arouse more nerves to begin with.

At the sides of her body, just below her underarms

This is a great teasing spot—you're not touching her breasts but you're arousing the nerve endings in that area, so she'll be getting really turned on. Touch her just above the skin. She has very fine golden hairs that you can't see, and as your fingers move over her skin they're stimulated, giving her a wonderful sensation.

Your Touch

Ask a woman if she'd rather have sex with a man whose hands were tied but whose penis was big or a man with a smaller than average penis whose hands were free, and I can guarantee that most would choose the second man. That's not to say size doesn't matter—it does—it's just that what you can do with your hands is more likely to bring her to orgasm.

Using your thumbs during kissing

Where you put your hands during a kiss can make or break the experience. Sometimes it's not your mouth or tongue that sends quivers down her spine, but the location of your fingers. Try sliding your hand up and down the sides of her upper body. The area just under her arm and by the sides of her breasts is incredibly sensitive, and being touched there will really turn her on. To improve further on this move, run your hands down her sides but let your thumbs take a more risqué route than your fingers and palm by pointing them in toward your body, so that they run very close to her breasts.

Tough touch or feather light?

There are times when a firm, even rough, touch can work without any preamble—but generally being teased first, aroused slowly, will make a woman (and man, incidentally) far more turned on. The longer you can build up the sexual tension, the greater her and your orgasm will be—because that's what an orgasm is, a release of that tension.

So how can you assess whether it's the right time for a fast and furious approach? As you're kissing or touching, speed it up just a little or apply a firmer touch—if she responds by pushing back at you harder, grabbing your behind just as firmly and pressing her lips hard against yours, then she's feeling just as sexually rowdy. But if you don't get that response, if she remains soft in your arms, maybe even slows down, then she's not ready for that level of touch yet. Take your time, keep touching her gently, maybe even pull away for a bit to tease her and get her revved up. Think of her as bread dough—she needs a bit of time gently warming to get aroused, before you give her a thorough kneading.

Making your hands look vulva-friendly

If a woman had dirty-looking teeth and chapped lips, would you want her mouth on your penis? Not likely. And that's why your hands need to be well looked after if you want to play with her erogenous zone. It's not just a question of looking groomed and like you care for yourself, a dirty fingernail or unwashed hand can give her a bladder infection. Many women have experienced cystitis at one time or another, and everyone who has will do what she can to make sure it doesn't happen again. Its symptoms include excruciating pain when she pees and a feeling of needing to pee all the time, and if it's left untreated, it can infect the kidneys, too. Although it is less common, cystitis can also affect men, so don't just think it's a problem for her. The best ways to avoid it is not to let anything dirty come into contact with her vagina (also a reason for never moving from her anus to vagina), and to pee before and after sex.

Use a scrubbing brush to get under your fingernails, and use hot soapy water. And wash them after you pee, too—hands up: who doesn't? You know who you are. The way you look after your hands says a lot to her about your overall hygiene, and if you want her to imagine your hands on her with a smile on her face, you'd better make sure you scrub up.

Digital manipulation, aka fingering her

I wish there was a more adult-sounding phrase to describe this sexual act, but "fingering" is what most of us immediately know and understand to be touching a woman with your fingers to bring her to orgasm. And this is where a little light reading of her women's magazines might come in handy. Since they're full of techniques to teach "your guy" and ways to a better orgasm, you'll learn a lot about her by leafing through her chick lit. But for now, here's some of the information you'll find in her magazines:

Her clitoris isn't just that little nub you can see; it extends a couple of inches inside her vagina—not down the vaginal canal where you put your penis, or your fingers, but around the outer lips (labia majora) in two "arms." So to get her really turned on and give her the equivalent of a warm-up hand job, you need to touch those parts. Stroke her lips from the bottom to the top as you would a cat's head, using several fingers at once; use one moistened finger to trace inside the outer lips, then inside the inner lips; use the palm of your hand on the entire lip area, rubbing gently. Hold the entire vulva in your hand with your palm on her pubic bone and pubic hair and your fingers facing down, covering her vaginal lips, and gently massage the area as though it were a soft, over-ripe furry peach that you'd like to squeeze just a little juice out of.

Have you got your finger on the button?

It's quite possible you're a bit off-center. You will have seen hundreds of other men's penises in changing rooms and toilets, but women have only rarely seen the same number of other women's clitorises—that means they have less knowledge about how different they are from other women. They may have no idea that they have a tiny clitoris, an unusually shaped one or a huge one. And until you've explored this particular woman you also won't know.

Some women have bright pink, pea-like clitorises that appear like a flower bud in spring when they're aroused; others have bean-sized ones that are visible even when they're not aroused; and others still have clitorises that never come out to play, they're so well-hidden under her skin.

How to locate any woman's clitoris

So first, let's describe exactly where a clitoris is and what form it takes. If you imagine a wishing bone from a chicken, you've got a pretty good approximation of the shape of a clitoris inside a woman. The apex of the bone represents the clitoris; the two "arms" extend back in toward her body and are "housed" inside her body. Locating a clitoris isn't difficult: run your fingers from the bottom of her vaginal lips, on the inside, until you get to the top where the inner lips join. Above the inner-lip join and below the outer-lip join is where you'll find the clitoris, a small nub of flesh that feels more solid that the surrounding skin when it's aroused. Some people describe it as feeling like a nose, but I think that's misleading as it sounds quite big and protruding—it can be tiny, or the size of a lentil, the size of a blueberry or even a broad bean. Whatever it feels like, it will always be located at the top of a woman's vaginal lips.

Search as you might, you cannot see her clitoris

It could be shy...The clitoris itself has a "foreskin"— this is the equivalent of your penis foreskin. Just like men, some women have big foreskins, whereas others have ones so tiny they're unnoticeable. This hood, as it's called, sometimes covers the clitoris when it's at its most aroused, to protect it, so don't be concerned if her clit is covered up. To manipulate or stimulate her clitoral hood, take her aroused clitoris gently between your finger and thumb and push back toward her body. You can also achieve this by pulling the skin back just above her clitoris with your thumb. Be extremely gentle. If you look, you will be able to see that you have pulled back some skin and her clitoris is revealed. But be aware that some women will love it if you now touch her clitoris directly whereas other women won't be able to handle such a direct touch. Many women prefer to be touched just above the clitoris, or to the sides.

One great rule to apply to all clitoral stimulation

Go gently and watch her response to see what she likes—she can always push her pubic area toward your hand, but it's more difficult for her to pull away, so always opt for a more gentle touch. Remember, the gentleman always gets the girl.

Deep-finger thrusting

How many times does your mom have to tell you? You should only play in the shallows. Well, maybe not all the time, but certainly when you're getting her warmed up (your girlfriend, not your mom). Only the outer third of the vagina has many nerve endings; deeper inside there's virtually no sensation at all, so your efforts deep down inside won't be having all that much effect. You can, however, try to stimulate her G-spot, a bundle of nerves about 2in up the front wall of her vagina. It doesn't do it for all women, but try rubbing your finger over the area, or pressing down on it gently—combined with stimulation on her clitoris, it can produce an astoundingly good orgasm. But don't be disappointed if it doesn't have the desired effect of helping her to orgasm—instead, focus your fingers' attention on the first 1in or so of her vaginal canal and her lips where she has more sensation.

When deep-finger thrusting is great

You may have read about "clitoral" and "vaginal" orgasms. This is a controversial differentiation because scientists are yet to prove that there's a quantifiable difference—especially now that they've discovered the clitoral arms extend quite far back into the woman's body. That said, penetrating her vagina may well give her a different orgasm from when you play with her clitoris alone.

It's all too easy to focus on the clitoris and forget to pleasure her elsewhere (a bit like if she concentrated on the head of your penis, without handling the rest of your shaft or fondling your balls, bum, and so on). So while you're fingering her clitoris, use your other hand to stimulate her vaginal lips and her vaginal canal.

Slide a finger inside her as you use your fingers on her clitoris, or use your thumb if it's easier. Use the same rhythm on her clitoris that you use inside her, and make sure you give her lips and the outer third of her vaginal canal lots of stimulation, as these are the parts with the most nerve endings.

The figure-eight technique

You've probably read about this trick. But, like licking the alphabet (see Chapter 5, page 104), it's by no means a guarantee for giving her an orgasm. The figure-eight technique, where you move around her clitoris in the pattern of an eight, will tease and excite a woman and possibly even bring her to orgasm, but for every woman who enjoys it, there'll be another who needs to have her clitoris rubbed like you're trying to remove paint off a door knob, and another who can only bear to have her clitoral sides touched, and yet another who needs a constant tapping to get her off. Every woman is different.

Clitoris finger moves

Here's a list of some techniques you can try. This list is not exhaustive, so experiment, mix them up, and enjoy the exploration:

- **Press and rub.** Using your palm, or the base of your fingers, you push against her clitoris and the surrounding area, making small movements up and down in a circular motion, as well as side to side.

- **Side massage.** Using your index finger and your third finger, locate the clitoris and put your fingers on either side of it. Now let your fingertips move up and down at the sides of her clitoris. If you do this with your fingers pointing toward her anus, try to feel for a muscle-like thread that leads toward the top of her vulva from her clitoris. This can be incredibly sensitive to touch and help her to orgasm.

- **Lip slide.** Put your third finger in between her inner lips—this only works if hers are at least ¼-½in with your index finger and ring finger on the outsides. This creates a kind of "lip sandwich.' Slide your hand up and down so that the base of your fingers is riding over her clitoris. Stimulating her inner lips like this feels fantastic.

- **Finger squeeze.** Some women can handle more clitoral stimulation than others, and if your woman's up for it, you can knead her clitoris between your thumb and index finger. It's incredibly intense and may well prove to be too much, so be careful.

When she's a palm-needer

A lot of women don't use their own fingers to bring themselves to orgasm, so why would yours work where hers can't? For these women, the palm of your hand, a flat vibrator or a pillow works far better than fingers because it stimulates a far bigger area—her vaginal lips as well as her clitoris.

Try a different method. If you're lying next to her, place your entire hand over her vulva with your fingers pointing down toward her behind. Using the heel of your hand, massage her clitoris along with the surrounding skin. For some women this is the best route to orgasm. If you're lying in between her legs, place your palm against her vaginal lips and massage her entire vulva with firm circular movements. When her head goes back and her back begins to arch as she thrusts toward you, you know you've got it right—from here on in, you're her treasured palm pilot.

Clitoral overkill

The clitoris is a fickle old thing—first it's too sensitive, but then, if you rub it too hard or for too long, it gets bored and loses sensation. It's almost as though the body shuts down nerve endings in the area because the sensation is too intense. This often happens if you start with a too-hefty touch, so always try to build up slowly. With the clitoris, less really is more to start with: feather-light touching with a well-lubricated finger, tracing your fingertips gently along her vaginal lips in between. This gets it truly ready for orgasm. Then gradually build up the pressure, but watch how she responds to make sure you don't apply too much pressure. If you're being too tender, she'll push against you or use her own hand over yours to show you how much pressure she needs. But it's always best to err on the side of too gentle because too forceful could result in no orgasm at all. Once the clitoris is desensitized, it'll take moving off completely before it is ready to become sensitive again, so focus on something else like playing with her breasts or nipples, or kissing, and then move back to stimulating it.

Finding the right rhythm

She knows you're a "handy man" to have around the house, but sometimes it's best to let her do the moving. In fact, if you're not sure how to bring your woman off, this is a great way to understand what kind of rhythm she likes and what pressure. Simply position your hand and fingers in such a way that your palm is touching her vaginal lips and your fingers are on her clitoris (you'll have to be lying in between her legs or low down on one side for this). Leave your hand there; don't move it around or push. If she really wants an orgasm, she'll push against your hand in the way that turns her on—just make sure you keep your hand in the same position. Let her do the moving, and keep your hand fixed in place. Her orgasm may not be entirely in your hands, but it will certainly be on your hand.

Don't stop using your hands

In the warm-up to penetrative sex and even the first few moments of it, you're very hands on, massaging breasts, squeezing her behind, and so on, but as soon as a you get close to climax, your hands turn to stone. The trouble is, she's probably getting close to orgasm at this point and needs the extra stimulation of your hands on her breasts, her hips, or her behind. Maintain your touching of her body throughout sex. It lets her know you're still finding her body a turn-on, but more importantly, it's what will help her reach orgasm herself.

Fingering the "other" hole

Gentle stimulation of her anal opening, or her "chocolate starfish" as friends of mine like to call it, can feel amazing. Some women will feel uncomfortable with this, whether it's for hygiene reasons—that is, they don't feel clean there or don't think it's hygienic for you to touch down there—or they just don't think it's "right" to mess with an anus. There are, however, good scientific reasons as to why it'll give her immense pleasure. The anus is packed with nerve endings (partly why going to the bathroom can give you a sensation of pleasure!), and if it's stimulated in the right way, can really add to her orgasm.

But, as we've said, it's really not for everyone and you can't make someone like it. Test the waters by first allowing your fingers to caress the area near her anus—not on or in it—and see how her body responds. Usually, if it's turning her on, she'll keep moving, maybe even thrust harder and push her behind toward your hand. If it's not doing anything for her, she's more likely to be startled, squeeze her butt cheeks together, or move your hand. Either way, leave your explorations at that for this session.

If that first foray went well, try putting your fingertip at the top of her anus so you're not quite touching it but you're close. But maybe save that move for the next sex session; it's important not to push on too quickly—that way she and you can get comfortable with what you're doing, learn to trust each other, and understand what works and what doesn't. Slow and steady is far more likely to give you both ulti-mate pleasure.

Next sex session, it's time to place your fingertip gently right on top of (but not inside) her anus. Massage it with your fingertip—this is sometimes all a woman needs to send her over the orgasmic edge. Having all these nerve endings stimulated along with her clitoris will give her an earth-shattering experience.

Going all the way in

If you want to put your finger inside, do it very carefully and with a well-lubricated finger. The tissue around the anus is very sensitive and tears easily, so fingernails should be neatly trimmed and filed (and use a pumice stone to get rid of those hard bits of skin at the corners of your nails, too). Start with just your fingertip inside, then, as she relaxes and enjoys it, put it in a little further. She has to be your guide in this, the slower you take it the more chance she has to respond and enjoy the sensation. Move too fast and you risk hurting her, her anal muscles clenching up and any sexy feelings totally lost. And always wash your hands before moving from her anus to her vagina, she can get a nasty infection otherwise—and scrub under your fingernails, too, as this is where most germs lurk. If that all sounds too much, use plastic wrap over the end of your finger. Keeping a wrap on things will help you both feel more comfortable.

Her Touch

How she touches you is important for your enjoyment of sex and that means it also affects how much she enjoys sex, so that's why I've included this section.

When she grabs you too hard

A lot of men go at it like a hammer trying to get a nail into wood when they're thrusting to climax during sex—she equates that to what she's doing and tries to match that same speed and pressure when she handles your penis. What she may not realize is that her vaginal canal isn't anywhere near as tight as a clenched fist on your manhood and you're the one who suffers because of it.

The other problem is that women are often told that they're too gentle (see below) and so they overcompensate to make sure that they're giving you maximum stimulation. There is an overwhelming school of thought that says, "Men need lots of fast and powerful pressure; women need a gentle, slow and soft touch." The fact is, there are women who need powerful pressure at high speed to orgasm and men who need slow, gentle thrusting to climax.

You've got to help her out here. First, hand her a big tube of lubricating jelly or oil. It's far more difficult to be rough or hurt someone when your hand is gliding smoothly over skin. Now place your hand over hers, slipping your fingers in between hers so you can ease her off your shaft, and show her how you like it. Keep your hand with hers the entire time to show her what pressure works, how fast you like it, and how fantastic it feels when you finally do climax.

When she's too gentle

We've read about "broken penises" in women's magazines, heard about women who were too firm with their hands, or worse, their teeth—and this is what makes her so namby-pamby in her touch. If she hasn't spent a lot of time playing, massaging, touching and fondling penises, she won't have been able to explore how soft, how hard, or what hurts and what doesn't. Again, it's up to you to show her. Place your hand over hers and apply as much pressure as you need.

Frenulum fear

Your frenulum—the piece of skin that attaches your foreskin to your penis—is terrifying to a woman. It looks like it'd snap under the slightest bit of pressure, and until a woman sees you masturbate and how frantically you probably move it back and forth, she won't really believe that it's as robust as it is.

Again, it's up to you to show her the way. Place your hand over hers and push down so that she understands that she can really move it quite a way down.

Hands-Solo Style

Masturbation is the Oh-ly Grail of great sex. It can solve so many problems, make things so much better, and even change your life—but it's an aspect of sex that we're just not taught about—not at school nor by our parents. This lack of education stems partly from the assumption that people know how to give themselves pleasure or because it's a sexual activity that most people don't boast about, so why try to improve on it?

I'll tell you why: you can have more control of your orgasms, even have bigger and better ones, and if you can discover how she masturbates, you can be a master of bringing her to orgasm, too.

What you can learn from her

Women can bring themselves to orgasm in a fraction of the time it takes to reach that same high during sex: on her own, knowing exactly what she wants and how to do it, it takes an average of three minutes; with you, it takes an average of 20 minutes. Wouldn't it be great if you could help her get to that oh-so-great place as quickly?

Finding out how she does it

Don't be surprised if she's reluctant to tell you how she masturbates—chances are, she thinks it's weird or abnormal. And that's because there isn't really a norm for her to follow. When a boy can first stand, he gets taught to hold his penis in his hand—so that he can pee standing up. Young girls, however, are taught to touch their vulvas only with tissue paper, when wiping after having been to the bathroom, and then to wash their hands immediately afterwards because they might be "dirty." Is it any wonder that most women don't come to masturbation easily and readily?

Assure her that you're open to whatever way she does it, but that you'd like to learn from watching and that it would turn you on to see her orgasm that way. If you mention that you know women do it in many different ways, she may well relax about telling you her method.

Watching her masturbate

This can be hugely educational and dramatically improve your sexual experience as a couple, but it can also be frustrating for you because it's sometimes difficult to see exactly what she's doing. Women's erogenous zones aren't as clear-cut as a chessboard—the clitoris varies from woman to woman, and the lips can be big, small, and different colors—in fact, all credit to men who find it with each new woman! Take an illustration of a woman's vulva and it looks fairly simple, but in reality, when everything's engorged with blood and changing color, and fingers are darting all over the place, well, it can be difficult to work out exactly what's going on.

So rather than make her feel totally self-conscious by pressing your nose right up against her thigh to get a good view, use your hands instead. Place your fingers gently on top of hers and feel what she's doing—getting the pressure and rhythm right will get you 99 percent of the way to bringing her off. You can then, perhaps, take over. Once you've got the right stroke rate, she can easily shift your hand or fingers up, down, left or right a bit to make sure you're in the right place and then leave you to it, if she wants to.

Simulating her masturbation technique

If she uses her fingers to masturbate, it's fairly straightforward to copy, but what if she uses something else—a pillow, for example? This is her way of stimulating the entire genital area, not just her clitoris, and if this is how she gets off, it's a good idea to try to stimulate her entire vulva when trying to get her off yourself. Use the palm of your hand to rub against her clitoris and the top of her vaginal lips, with your fingers playing on the lower part of her lips. Slide your fingers up and down her vaginal lips, with her lips slipped between your fingers—this is a fantastic way to stimulate all of her clitoris.

Improving *your* masturbation technique

Think you can't improve your self-love? Think again.

Showing her how you do it

You'll read advice about how watching a woman masturbate is a great way to understand how to bring her to orgasm—so why not place the same emphasis on watching a man give himself pleasure? Male masturbation in films or in writing is often depicted as a frantic under-the-sheets affair, whereas seeing a woman do the same thing is usually sensuously illustrated, lovingly lit and photographed. And yet, watching how a man brings himself to orgasm can be a huge turn-on and also very informative—if you're both willing to give it a go. Often couples will discover that their partner uses different techniques to reach orgasm than those they use during sex, and you can both use that new knowledge to your advantage in the bedroom.

If watching each other is too full-on, and too intimate an experience, do it by touch instead. Blindfold yourselves and then masturbate, feeling the other person's hands to understand the rhythm, the intensity, and the strength of their touch. Often, when mutually masturbating, you'll end up having sex anyway. But who's complaining?

Changing your solo style

If hard and fast is what gets you to orgasm quickest, try changing your technique. It will help make sex more pleasurable for her—as she'll enjoy firm, constant pressure. And taking your time—holding back, then letting go, then holding back again—can teach you to separate ejaculation from orgasm, potentially leading to multiple orgasms for you, without losing your erection. Try this method:

1. **Week one.** Time yourself to discover how long you take to reach a climax, on average. Let's say it's four minutes. For the first week, masturbate with a dry hand, holding off from ejaculation until you can go for 15 minutes before shooting your load.

2. **Week two.** Add a lubricant and build up to 15 minutes again.

3. **Week three.** Keep practicing with the lubricant—go back to doing it dry if you find you can't. Build up to 20 minutes.

4. **Week four.** Add some kind of visual stimulus to the mix: use your imagination or look at your favorite porn magazine or film. Keep practicing until you can do 20 minutes with all stimuli.

5. **Week five.** Now focus on your breathing. As you get closer to climax, slow your breathing down and make it much deeper. Focus on the sensation in your penis, and when you feel you're about to blow, stop and breathe. This is one way you can learn to differentiate between the feeling of orgasm and ejaculation itself. And if you don't get to be a multiorgasmic guy, you've had a lot of fun trying!

Real Girls Tell All

SHARON tells how she likes to be handled:

"I love to have my breasts massaged. I think I could probably orgasm from that feeling alone if it went on long enough. My fella puts loads of cocoa butter lotion in his hands and says he's going to moisturize me. He'll start at my feet, work his way up my legs to my stomach, then along my arms—he'll touch everywhere except my breasts, then finally he'll use his palms just to touch my nipples, which are erect by now. He moves over them making circles, then pushes down harder and moves in circles all around them. It feels absolutely amazing."

HANNAH on how she likes to be fingered:

"The boyfriend I'm with now is amazing with his fingers. He's a guitar player, not sure if that's got anything to do with it, but he manages to keep the pressure up for ages and that's what I need. He uses his first two fingers and keeps them close together and then rubs the tips of them over and over my clitoris, again and again until I come."

STELLA on how she likes to be touched:

"The softest, lightest touch turns me on more than any other way of touching. If I've had a shower and I've dusted myself with talc it feels the most amazing because my husband's fingers move over my body so smoothly, gliding over my dry skin. He makes patterns on my body, circles on my breasts, strokes on my inner thighs, zigzags over my belly. It feels lovely because he's loving every part of me, exploring my skin as though he's not seen it before. He knows how much I love it, that's why he does it, but I'm sure he gets a kick out of it, too, because he always has a wonderful big erection, which we put to good use!"

8

Sex toys

Sex toys have really come out of the closet in the last ten years—thousands of vibrators are sold every day online, but it's not just there: "high-street" stores now also sell small vibrators, ribbed condoms, and lubricants. And hooray for that, because in the right hands, a vibrator, a dildo, or a spot of lube can do amazing things for both women and men.

Introducing Toys

Just as most men would run a mile if they were led into a woman's bedroom that featured a display of stuffed animals, most women will get spooked if you show them any type of sex toy—including lubrication—on the first night. Learn about sex toy etiquette before you show and tell.

Showing her what's in your bedside drawers

If you're entangled in each other's naked bodies, and you reach over to grab your conveniently placed baby oil/flavored lube/fluffy handcuffs, be prepared for some screaming. Not ecstatic orgasmic screaming, mind, but mad, angry-woman screaming. Why? Because it looks as though (a) you've done this with one or more women before; and (b) you knew she would sleep with you tonight so you were prepared. While she no doubt knows you've had sex with other people before, she doesn't want to have her face rubbed in the knowledge just as she's warming up for sex. She's also likely to be less than delighted that her jumping into bed with you was predictable.

As a general rule, avoid using sex toys or aids on a first night. Of course, if you're with a wild sex kitten or you've been with this woman for a while, feel free to keep a sack-load of sex toys and lubes next to your bed—but never, ever give the impression that they may have been used with someone else.

Toys, especially cheaply made ones with ridges that catch juices, hair, and skin, can harbor all kinds of bacteria. Always follow the instructions on the sex toy when cleaning it. And forget what your parents told you—it's never nice to share your toys.

Your love of butt play

Butt plugs sell in huge quantities on sex toys' websites and shops, and yet 95 percent of men would rather die than admit they enjoy a bit of anal play. For this reason, most women aren't aware of the extreme pleasure they can give a man with some anal stimulation. If you've invested in a butt plug, and you whip it out during sex, she's quite likely to think you plan to use it on her. The notion of a man already being aware of the pleasure zone a couple of inches inside his anus—the prostate—is in itself a little startling to most women. So the introduction of a butt plug or even anal stimulation may have your good lady running scared.

Women are often wary of putting their finger, or anything else, near your anus because of hygiene issues. Men also tend to have more hair in their cracks, and that makes it even less appealing (dangleberries, anyone?). So apart from washing well and possibly even going for a crack-wax (or use depilatory cream if that's too much to bear), suggest she use a bit of clear plastic wrap over her finger—or she can even wear a rubber glove. It'll give her more confidence while stimulating you, and, with a bit of lube, should make the experience more sensuous for you.

Fear of big vibrators

Don't be scared of her vibe, even if it is 10in long, bright pink and spinning around faster than a disco ball. Vibes tend to be shaped like penises and yet most women will use a vibrator not to penetrate but to stimulate the clitoris directly—they could be shaped like a cup or a football and still do a similar job.

What's more, her vibrator is your best friend in the bedroom. Not only will it bring her to orgasm faster because of its intense pulsating, which stimulates her nerve endings more efficiently, but it will also heighten your pleasure because it allows you to have sex in positions that don't usually bring a woman to orgasm. For example, if you're doing it on all fours, a vibrator held against her clitoris means you can both enjoy the position; otherwise her clitoris gets no stimulation whatsoever. For spooning, the vibe can be slipped between her legs, stimulating her clitoris and lips as well as your penis and testicles. And in missionary, she can place the vibrator underneath your penis, giving you an intense buzz while transforming your manhood into a vibrating rocket. Far out.

Choosing a vibrator

The thing that often puts men off vibrators is their obvious phallic shape—why would a man want to give his girlfriend another longer, harder penis to use? So go for a different shape—get yourselves a fingertip vibrator or one that's pebble-shaped. Then it's even easier to use it everywhere—on your nipples or hers, at the top of your buttocks (a very sensitive area), on your perineum (the area between your anus and testicles), and up and down your shaft. Use lubrication and the experience is guaranteed to be sensational.

Dildos can also be useful

Phallic-shaped toys that don't necessarily vibrate are called dildos and are for penetration—if the dildo's inside her vagina, you won't be. So it's understandable that you might feel a bit put out if she pulls one out (especially if it's on the larger side). But, like vibrators, dildos can also be used in a couple situation: they can be used to stimulate her to orgasm before you have sex together—some women enjoy the feeling of having something inside them while their clitoris is licked or played with, using a dildo allows her to enjoy both. Visually, it can be a fantastic turn-on for you, too, so don't knock it till you've tried it.

The dildo-wielding woman in your bed may also enjoy being penetrated simultaneously in her anus and vagina. But whatever it is she wants you to do with her dildo, you need guidance—don't assume you know what she wants. Let her tell you or show you how she likes it to be used, otherwise you may well end up barking up the wrong tree, or heading down the wrong rabbit hole.

Using Toys

Just like penises and vaginas, vibrators and cock rings, and so on, can be successfully used or abused—make sure you're using yours to the best of your ability.

Vibrating penis ring: the best sex toy there is

The vibrating cock ring has revolutionized both on-all-fours sex and missionary sex. It's a simple elasticized ring, with a tiny vibe on one side designed to stimulate the clitoris. With the vibe positioned either on the underside of the penis for doggy-style or on top for missionary, it's one of the few vibrators that's easy to use during penetrative sex. It's non-threatening because it's not phallic. There's no need to hold it in place and it allows for complete penis penetration, unlike other non-phallic vibrators, which are too big or awkwardly shaped to allow for body-on-body sex.

But not so great if she's sensitive

The trouble with the fantastic penis ring is that not all women can handle the intensity of such direct stimulation. Particularly if you're using the penis ring in missionary, where all your weight is going into the thrusting and each time that powerful little vibe is knocking right on her clitoral door. For doggy-style, however, it should be perfect, as it doesn't push so forcefully on her sensitive clitoris. Experiment with different positions until you get it right.

You in handcuffs

If your girlfriend rarely orgasms, but she masturbates regularly and successfully, this can be a great opportunity for her to find ways to get herself to climax while having sex with you. Often a woman is so intent on her partner's pleasure that she neglects her own: being in full control might encourage her to think more selfishly. It's also a great way to discover the kind of rhythm, pressure, and technique that she enjoys.

For those women who are overly focused on their partner's pleasure, however, handcuffing you can put even greater pressure on her to perform—to bring you to orgasm. After all, your hands are tied, so everything—from technique to rhythm to how often touch or speed is varied—is down to her. It's like being put in the driver's seat and being told to find your way to Climax House—what if she gets lost on the way? To avoid this kind of performance anxiety, make it clear that you don't want to reach climax while you're tied up. That way, she'll feel relaxed about doing what she feels comfortable doing, safe in the knowledge that she's not expected to "finish the job." If she happens to bring you to climax while you're cuffed, all the better.

Her in handcuffs

Again, because many women are intent on their partner's pleasure, giving up control like this can also help. But it must be something she wants to try. Many women gain pleasure by being dominated by a man, to feel small and less powerful, but it's not for everyone.

If you're introducing the idea to her, start with innocent-looking handcuffs—pink, fluffy ones, or Velcro ones that can be undone easily. This is preferable to using a silk scarf or a pair of her tights, as often recommended—a tight knot in a pair of nylons is near impossible to free yourself from and you want her to feel lightly restrained, not totally immobilized. Trust is an obvious element of this sex "game," so be careful—if she shows any sign of discomfort with being tied up or whatever you're doing, stop immediately.

You may have different ideas from her about what's OK in this "sex play" and be unaware that you're taking things too far. That's why it is absolutely essential to use a code word such as "Coventry" or something equally non sexual whenever indulging in sex that involves restraints or pain—pleasure techniques such as spanking, for example. Saying, "Ow" could be taken as a good "Ow" or a bad "Ow"—how are you to know which it is? Similarly with restraints, it's important you have a code for when you or she really wants the restraints to be removed.

Finally, I know it sounds obvious, but never, ever leave a partner restrained in a room, even if you're just heading to the toilet. I've been told several stories about this kind of thing going horribly wrong, and let me tell you, it's enough to put you off for life.

Lubricator: the essential sex toy

Once seen as something older women or gay men needed, lubrication is now, thankfully, easily available, and all kinds of lubes are now sold, in different flavors, textures and chemical make-up. Don't focus on lubrication as being something to fix a problem (that is, her dryness); see it as oil for her engine: it simply makes her parts, and yours, run more smoothly. Adding a squirt of lubrication to proceedings speeds up the arousal process—partly because the sensation of something wet between her legs feels damned sexy but also, I believe, because it cons the body into feeling like it's already ready for sex.

For a woman, there are few things less sexy than having a man put his hands or penis between your legs only for it to chafe or rub hard because you're dry down below. All the more disappointing if you feel really horny, but for some reason you're just not moist—something that's happened to many, if not all, women at some stage or another. She may feel utterly horny but still the juices just won't flow. It could be that she's stressed and not relaxed enough, that she hasn't drunk enough water that day, or simply that she's drunk too much alcohol, which has dehydrated her body. Whatever the reason, if she feels turned on and wants to continue, lubrication is the answer.

Note: Be aware that some lubes may not be safe to use with condoms. Always check the label.

Using a vibrator: on her
Try not to dive straight in, homing in on her clitoris straight away. Tease her a little, move it over her belly, her inner thighs, her breasts, her nipples (using

lube makes it even sexier), and so on, before getting fixated on her vulva. Once you're in between her legs, move the vibe up and down her lips to get her clitoris (which, remember, has "arms" that extend into her body) really excited. Then, if she can handle it, focus on the clitoris.

As with your tongue or finger, holding a vibrator in place is often the best way to get her to orgasm. Rather than trying to move the stimulator—be it finger, tongue, or vibe—as you guess she might like it, she gets to control the move. Hold it steady and in one place and watch as her hips rotate to grind against it. You can learn far more by watching how she does it than you will by trying to show her how you think it'll work best for her—after all, she's probably been practicing on herself for as many years as you've been playing with yourself. Freeze your position and the experience may well be a lot hotter for her.

Using a vibrator: on you

Vibrators are not just for her, they're equally amazing for you; it all depends on how you use them. For example, if she holds it against your testicles and the underside of your penis during missionary, you'll get a wonderful buzzing sensation as you thrust in and out. If she twirls a vibe-tip over your lubricated nipples when she's grinding away on top of you, you'll get huge nerve stimulation. Best of all, if she places the pulsating vibrator on the side of her cheek as she goes down you, you'll get a vibrating blow job. What the vibrations do is tickle and stimulate more nerve endings than through touch alone—it wobbles and vibrates the entire skin area as well as underneath the skin, so you're triggering more sensation and therefore more arousal. Lucky you.

Household Objects

Some of the best things to play with in bed don't have to be bought from a sex shop. Here are some everyday objects you can use to make your sex life better.

Ripe peaches and nectarines

Most women love to play with fruit and food in bed. It's messy, but it's very, very sensual. Bringing the sense of taste into the bedroom adds to the experience and I think, in part, using fruit or food to lick each other makes women feel more comfortable about oral sex—whether it's giving or receiving it.

Peaches make great fellatio fruits: simply core as you would an apple, then slide over the penis. Massage the peach as she sucks and licks on your penis. Eventually the peach will disintegrate but now your penis tastes just peachy so she can get really busy eating you.

Ice cream

Get her one from the ice cream truck, but while you're there, get an extra cone as well as another ice cream and then put it to good use in the bedroom. Bite off the end of the cone, slide it over your penis and then plop the ice cream on top—then tell her you've got an ice cream for her, only she has to eat it off you. This is really good fun, again very messy, but a great way to enjoy ice cream on a hot day.

Can of beer

Beer is sexy after all! On a hot day, take any cold can from the fridge and roll it up and down the back of her bare legs. Then turn her over and roll it gently over her nipples, move down to her stomach and give her inner thighs a cold tingle, too. A wonderfully refreshing way to get sexually hot on a summer's day.

The car

Fumbling teenage experiences don't count—doing it properly in a car is incredibly sexy and erotic, maybe in part because of teenage experiences. But don't try doing it in the front where the gearshift, steering wheel, and dashboard get in the way terribly; instead, head to the back seat, open one car door, and have her leave her legs hanging there. You should be able to get reasonably comfortable on top. It's hot, it's heavy, and it's a lot of good fun.

Another position to try, if you're somewhere no one can see you, is the window seat. She rests her behind on the wound-down side-window of the car (feet on the floor), as you stand by the car and penetrate her from there. It's outside sex but without the ants in your pants or the effort of supporting her weight.

A blanket or pillow

When it comes to her orgasm, it's all about the angle, and in the missionary position her clitoris sometimes doesn't quite get enough stimulation. But there's a solution to that little problem—a solution that comes in all shapes and sizes. A cushion, a pillow, or a rolled-up blanket will do the trick—simply put it under her bottom. What this does is raise her pelvis toward yours, so that each time you thrust there's more contact with her clitoris and also her vaginal lips. Whatever method you use to raise your game, not only will she enjoy the discovery process as she gets closer to orgasm but she'll also appreciate your new found interest in upholstery.

Books

Women spend a lot of their time imagining and talking about scenarios, what-ifs, and maybes. That means she probably has ideas about sex that you don't even know about. And a great way to explore her mind—or indeed fill it—is to read with her. There are hundreds of authors who spend their time creating sexy, erotic stories for women (and for men) and whereas not all will be to her taste, there's bound to be one that gets her excited. But it's not just about the style, it's about how the information is relayed: by reading an erotic story she can imagine the woman and the man (if she wants, it can be you and her), but whoever the characters are, she chooses how they look, which makes it more personal than a porn film. Some books also have fantastic storylines, which encourage overall enjoyment of reading, with hot sex scenes woven expertly in. This is such a good way to open up her mind to new ideas and also to discover things she may enjoy that you don't yet know about.

Stairs

The most under-used sex toy in the house must be the stairs. You can stand at the bottom as she sits a few steps up, giving you exactly the vantage point you need. She can kneel on the stairs as you take her from behind, standing up. You can sit on the stairs with her sitting on you and facing away from you as she thrusts up and down on to you, holding on to the banisters for support.

Real Girls Tell All

RACHEL explains her love for her vibrator:

"I didn't know whether I'd even had an orgasm when my friend bought me my first vibe. It was a silly-looking "real life" penis. I took it home and chucked it into a side drawer and forgot about it, but then months later when I was looking for something else, I found it. I must have been feeling horny because I decided to see what it felt like. My God, I wish someone had held me down and made me use it years before! It felt so, so good immediately. I'd tried to masturbate with my fingers before but I got tired too fast; with the vibrator I could just let it do all the work."

GABY describes her ultimate sex-toy experience:

"Food, food, food. I had the best sex I've ever had with my boyfriend one day when we were making blueberry and raspberry tarts—they had a pastry base, with a custard filling and the fruit on top. We were in the kitchen and were getting the dough ready for the pastry when he flicked a bit of flour on my face. I flicked back and soon it was an all-out flour fight. I added water, which would have been a mistake, but he found it funny and we both looked such a mess. Then he started wiping the custard on my face, I did the same and got him on the neck. Then we started on the fruit. We laughed so hard, then we started kissing and even with all the floury bits it tasted good. We ended up licking custard off each other on the kitchen floor. It was a wild, wild time."

DIANNE describes what she does to her boyfriend with her sex toy:

"First I rub massage oil all over his body so the vibrator runs smoothly. I use a vibrating massager so it covers quite a large area. I start on his feet, which tickles him a bit, then I work up his lower legs, concentrating on his calf muscles. I move it over his upper legs and his abs and his arms. He loves it on his nipples, so I leave that 'til last—it makes him moan when I get there. Then while I'm doing that, I start massaging his balls in my hands; then I use the vibe down there—that sends him insane. I keep it there while I go down on him. He comes really quickly when I do the whole process like that. I think it's because it heats him up for the action!"

9

Sex fantasies

Thinking about sex certainly makes you want it more. It's partly why the first few months of sex with a new partner are so amazing—you spend most of your time when you are apart thinking about what you'll do to each other when you see them. And that's why fantasies and sexual daydreams are great. It's whether or how we put them to use that can cause problems.

When most people hear the term "sexual fantasies" they think of unusual or clichéd sex fantasies—orgies, doctors and nurses, or whip-wielding dominatrixes. But according to a survey of more than 6,000 people by *Men's Health* magazine, the most common sexual daydream for both genders is far more mundane—it's simply good sex with their partner. Don't rest on your sexual laurels just yet, though—you're both fantasizing about good sex, but you might not be getting what you want in bed. And that's where fantasies can help, if you share them.

Her Fantasies

The devil's in the detail, and never more so than when it comes to women's sexual fantasies. Elaborate storylines, perfectly imagined looks and an exact touch-by-touch process is what gets a lot of women to orgasm.

The "clean-living, filthy-thinking woman"

The notion of the uptight and prim woman who goes wild behind closed doors is your fantasy. Yes, some women may well have repressed sexual feelings that explode once you get them into bed, but it's certainly no guarantee. Repressing your sexual feelings isn't healthy, and I'd hope that most women these days realize that enjoying sex is a good thing, not something to be ashamed of.

The other common misconception is that you can turn your "good girl bad." It's an idea based on the notion that experimenting, loving and wanting sex is "bad." And while being "bad" is something some women may aspire to, it supports the idea that women are naturally less inclined to want sex and that that's how they're meant to behave. Please! Time to drop this notion once and for all—women love sex, want sex, and enjoy sex just like you do; it's just that we've had years of social conditioning telling us it's "bad." Stop!

Her secret fantasies

You'll be surprised at what goes on in 49 percent of women's minds. According to a *Cosmopolitan* poll, that's the percentage of women who dream about sex with their partner. Sweet. But before you settle into feeling smug, consider this: most of those women tend to fantasize about situations or sex acts they don't usually enjoy with their partners. If only you could find out what her fantasies were...

Talking about her fantasies

You can't read her mind and you'd be a fool to try to guess: the best method to get her to open up is to show and tell yourself. Tell her about a "dream" you've had, detailing sex with her; if she's got any fantasies she'd like to share, this gives her a perfect opportunity to reveal all.

If that doesn't work, you'll have to try playing a game—telling her your fantasies in exchange for hers. But rather than jump in there with, "You, dressed as a nurse and I'm your sick patient"—she probably already knows how much you love to be nursed—play a game that allows you both to explore different possible fantasies. Each write down a list of ten fantasies, not your fantasies, just sex acts or scenes that could happen. Make at least five of them acts that you're not interested in, and the other five ones that you are. Then go through each of them, talking about whether you would want to try any of them. By including fantasies you're not really interested in, it takes the pressure off, as it allows either party to expose their secret fantasies without being laughed at and without shocking their partner.

Her favorite fantasy: the fireman

According to the aforementioned poll, women's number-one situational fantasy is that she's trapped in a building and you're a fireman who rescues her. Uniforms, phallic water-hoses and hard helmets aside, what's the attraction? This is an extra-safe form of a domination fantasy. When the woman is rescued by the fireman, he has total control of the situation and she is vulnerable. She experiences fear, which heightens her senses, but her fear is of the fire, not of him. Then he saves her—and now she feels indebted to him, too, setting a perfect scenario for a steamy lovemaking session.

So how can you make her fantasy come true without the very real—and highly un-erotic—danger of a fire? You can't rescue her from something genuinely terrifying, but you can rescue her from her day-to-day life. Rescue her from the shopping, from her hard day at work, or from her nightmare relative—take control of a difficult situation and make it better. If it doesn't have the effect of making her tear off your clothes and leap into bed, at least she'll be grateful for your help—and in the long run that will equate to more loving for you.

Her most realistic fantasy: outdoor sex

Public sex is the experimental sex most women would like to try, according to the same poll mentioned earlier, with 74 percent saying they'd give it a go. But forget the toilets, the local park, or bus shelter—it's far more likely she's thinking about the beach, which was the favorite fantasy location for women.

Sex on the beach has been made desirable in numerous films, as well as a rather delicious cocktail, but in reality it can be downright uncomfortable. Sand in your sandwiches is one thing, but sand sandwiched in your salami or her burger buns is an entirely different thing! The key to making it romantic—and successful—involves taking adequate protection. And I'm not just talking condoms—it goes without saying that you should use those. You need to take a waterproof-backed blanket, because that's the best way to ensure sand doesn't work its way through and it keeps you both warm, too; you'll also need a windbreak, not just to protect you from the breeze but also from prying eyes. Finally, don't forget to put suntan lotion on your sensitive parts—you don't want to burn your behind.

Her secret fantasy: erotica

There's a good chance that fantasizing about nudity is a big part of her arousal when masturbating—and that looking at erotica turns her on, much as it does for many men. However, she may not even realize that she's aroused by looking at naked bodies. According to one university study, even those women who claimed they were not turned on by erotic films displayed signs of arousal, such as engorged genitals and lubrication, when shown such films. But don't be surprised if your personal DVD collection does nothing but disgust her—pornography is usually designed along very specific lines: lots of close-up shots of genitalia, women who enjoy being penetrated from every possible angle and from any man, however unattractive, and virtually no story line. It rarely touches on the many different factors that are involved in the sex we enjoy in a relationship—the build-up, tension, different rhythms and speeds, varying techniques and ways of touching, scenarios and situations, and, of course, emotions. And before you scoff at emotions being important to great sex, think about the best orgasm you've ever had. Was it while watching porn? Was it on a one-night stand? Most likely, it was with someone you cared about. That's emotions for you—so powerful they give you better orgasms.

The kind of erotica she's more likely to enjoy

As I've said, pornography is very much about the sex act, rather than the lead-up or emotions involved—and women can find this aspect of it off-putting. It also often presents an unrealistic picture of sex: soft lighting, models' buff bodies, and camera angles make everyone look fantastic. And just as you will probably compare the size of your penis to the guy's on the DVD, she'll be comparing herself to the women she sees—which can lead to insecurities.

For these reasons, it's imperative that you allow her to lead the way when viewing erotica. If she's comfortable with the idea, let her choose what to watch. Women haven't grown up with a culture of watching erotica, unlike many men, so give her time to find her feet, discover what she likes and what she doesn't. And if she decides the magazine or DVD is not for her, respect her decision.

If you're not even sure whether she'd like any erotica, start with a beautiful coffee-table photography book, or watch a film with sensuous scenes in it—there are plenty of both that are considered art rather than pornography and it's a good way to gauge her response to the naked form.

Another of her favorite fantasies: girl on girl

Dipping a toe in the lesbian lake holds far less fear for women than a homosexual experience does for men—as many as 61 percent of women in a poll by erotic magazine *Scarlet* said they'd like to give it a try. Full steam ahead then? Not so fast, sailor. This isn't a fantasy about threesomes, it's a fantasy about lesbian sex—and that may well not include you.

If her lesbian fantasy doesn't include you, do keep in mind that it is a fantasy; just as you probably have sexual daydreams that you don't actually want to follow through, so may she. If, however, your girlfriend wants to make her lesbian daydreams a reality but doesn't want you to be part of them, then you have to question her commitment to you. It doesn't matter what gender the other person is—by having sex with another person you are changing the status of your relationship.

Her pain fantasy: a little bit of slap 'n' tickle

She may fantasize about being lightly spanked, having her hair tugged, or even being bitten. These acts all have the effect of bringing blood to the surface, which makes the area even more sensitive to touch (unless you overdo it and the area becomes numb). Making this fantasy a reality is relatively easy, but, as I've mentioned previously, it's essential you use a code word to say "stop" to ensure you don't cause her real pain.

Your Fantasies

OK, so enough about her, what about you? Your fantasies aren't all that different from hers, according to surveys, but there are still things you'd like to have a go at and she certainly has issues with some of your sexual daydreams. Find out what they are here.

Telling her about your fantasies

So she's asked you to tell her what you fantasize about—be very careful! Women think they want to know everything—I do—but in reality we really don't want to hear that you fantasize about having sex with anyone younger, prettier, or more exciting than us. (Or anyone older, uglier, or more boring—that's just weird.) Test the waters by telling her you've had a strange sexual dream—it's the easiest and safest way to gauge her response.

If you do talk about it and your fantasies are more hardcore than she expected, she may question how much satisfaction you get in bed with her—even though you may not want to act out your fantasies with her or anyone else. If, for example, you like to imagine having sex like a Hell's Angel on a Harley and you usually do it in bed when she's got her "good" white nightie on, then she'll feel stupid for thinking you had a good sex life—she will think that you've been wishing she'd get a tattoo, start drinking beer, and swear profusely. So opt for telling her fantasies that are more racy versions of what you do already, rather than radically different new acts.

One of your favorite fantasies: threesomes

It's not one of the most common fantasies for women, but one in four say they'd like to try having a threesome, according to one magazine poll. Before you get too excited, though, be aware that the poll didn't specify whether women wanted a threesome with their partner and another female, or a partner and another male. Don't assume her threesome fantasy is the same as yours!

Putting a fantasy like this into reality is risky: most couples who try it find it affects their relationship in a negative way, mainly because it introduces insecurities and jealousies. Possibly one of her—and your—fantasies that's best left as that.

The fantasy you must never share: another woman

Whereas the majority of people in couples have loving erotic daydreams about their partners, 15 percent of men and 12 percent of women fantasize about random strangers; 20 percent of men and 15 percent of women think about a friend; and a further 15 percent of men and 11 percent of women do the downright dirty and fantasize about their ex. Is it a problem to think about someone else while you're sexually ruminating? No, it's really not. We dream about a lot of things we don't actually need or want in reality—and it's the same for our sexual dreams. When it does become a problem, however, is if you are having to think of someone you know in order to orgasm when you're with your partner or while masturbating. You are effectively replacing your partner with that person, and that indicates that you're not really physically or emotionally attracted to the person you're with. But there's no doubt about whether or not you should let her in on any of these "other women" fantasies: no, no, and no. Some secrets should stay that way.

Your fun fantasy: costumes

Most women love to get dressed up, but that love may not stretch to include a policewoman's or a nurse's outfit. Unless you know for sure that she's up for acting out the part of Officer Pussy or Nurse Naughty, the worst thing you can do is to go out and buy her an outfit as a surprise. Instead, peruse an online sex-toy shop together—most have a full range of products, from condoms, lubes, vibrators and French maid outfits to chastity belts, anal beads, and latex body suits. She can pick something she'd like to wear, rather than you surprising her with an outfit that'll stay at the back of her cupboard, never to see the light of day or night.

Want to live the dream?

If you do choose to act out any of her or your fantasies, be aware that it's highly likely to be a disappointment. It's not unusual for a favorite daydream to come true, only for the dreamer to find it wasn't quite as wonderful as they expected: that job you've always wanted turns out to be hell on earth; the woman you thought you loved turns out to be a raging maniac; the tranquil beach holiday you booked features irritating flies and tourists that weren't in the brochure description. And it's exactly the same with sexual fantasies—often, they're best left just as they are: as thoughts that inspire you or her.

If you do have an experience that doesn't work out as planned, assuage each other's disappointments by having good, loving sex... soon after. It's a good way to ensure the intimacy you feel during sex hasn't been lost or replaced by the other experience.

Real Girls Tell All

CHRISTINE describes her fantasy about being dominated:

"I find it really difficult to relax and enjoy sex. I just can't stop thinking about my husband's pleasure and whether he's really enjoying it, and that stops me from being able to focus on what makes me come. I've never had an orgasm during penetrative sex, although I'm sure I could if I could just relax. That's why when I masturbate I imagine that he pins me down, won't let me move my arms—he holds them together above my head, and he uses his other hand to hold my hips in place. Then he grinds into me, pushing right on my clitoris and I don't have any choice but to come."

DEBORAH describes her flower fantasy:

"I've always wanted to do it in a field of flowers, but in my fantasy, we're doing it, the man I'm with has pulled my dress up and we're hot and sweaty, and then we hear the grass around us rustling, like someone's walking nearby. The man I'm with stops, stays inside me, but stops. We both wait and don't hear anything and then the man I'm with slowly starts thrusting again, but this time without so much movement, just deeper inside me. We're still being really quiet. We hear more footsteps. It carries on like that, stopping and starting, not knowing if those footsteps are going to get closer and we'll be found."

WANDA describes her anal fantasy: NO

"My husband and I have great sex but for some reason we've never explored anal stimulation and it's a bit of a disappointment to me. I feel it's a bit too late now to suggest it! So anyway, in my fantasy, my husband and I are about to have dinner in a restaurant. I'm wearing a long dress that is very low-cut at the back. As we get to the table, he pulls out my chair and inadvertently puts his thumb down the back of my dress and touches my bottom. It feels so good that I shudder and he notices. All through dinner I'm excited and as we leave to go to the car, he lets his hand slide down to my bottom again. By now I'm very, very wet and desperate to get home. But on the drive home he doesn't touch me. I'm squirming on the seat with anticipation but wondering if he'll know what to do when we get in the door.

"He closes the door behind him, goes to take my coat off so I turn my back to him. He lets the coat fall and rubs his stubbly chin all the way from the back of my neck down my back to my bottom. There, he grinds his chin into the top of my bottom, then kisses it, then licks it until suddenly his tongue is inside my anus. I'm already exploding when he moves the palm of his hand under me and onto my clitoris and pushes on it—as he does that, he pushes my bottom into his tongue even further, it's the most delicious thing I've ever felt. Then I come. And wow, it's the best orgasm in the world."

References

If you require sources for any of the polls or studies mentioned, or contact details of any experts I have quoted, please contact me via my website www.siski-green.com and I will deal with requests as and when I am able.

Books
Brief Encounters: the women's guide to casual sex
Emily Dubberley, Fusion Press, London, 2005

How to Give Her Absolute Pleasure: totally explicit techniques every woman wants her man to know
Lou Paget, Piatkus, London, 2002

How to Have Great Sex for the Rest of Your Life
Val Sampson & Julia Cole, Piatkus, London, 2004

How to Tell a Naked Man What to Do: sex advice from a woman who knows
Candida Royalle, Piatkus, London, 2006

My Secret Garden: women's sexual fantasies
Nancy Friday, Quartet Books, London, 2001

O: the intimate history of the orgasm
Jonathan Margolis, Century, London, 2004

Overcoming Sexual Problems
Vicki Ford, Constable and Robson, London, 2005

Scentsational Sex: the secret to using aroma for arousal
Alan R Hirsch, MD, Element, London, 2005

Sex Etiquette for Ladies and Gentlemen
Em & Lo, Hodder and Stoughton, London, 2005

Sex for Dummies
Dr. Ruth K. Westheimer, Hungry Minds, New Jersey, 2006

She Comes First: the thinking man's guide to pleasuring a woman
Ian Kerner, PhD, Souvenir Press, London, 2005

Sinful Sex: the uninhibited guide to erotic pleasure
Dr. Pam Spurr, Robson Books, London, 2002

Superdate: how to be one, how to get one
Tracey Cox, Dorling Kindersley, London, 2006

The Big O: how to have them, give them and keep them coming
Lou Paget, Piatkus, London, 2002

The Book of the Penis
Maggie Paley, Fusion Press, London, 1999

Tickle Your Fancy: a woman's guide to sexual self-pleasure
Sadie Allison, Tickle Kitty Press, San Francisco, 2001

Websites

www.2magazine.ca
(online branch of 2 magazine,
Canadian magazine for couples)

www.bbc.co.uk/relationships
(BBC's emotional issues online)

www.cosmopolitan.co.uk
(online branch of *Cosmopolitan* magazine UK)

www.cosmopolitan.com
(online branch of *Cosmopolitan* magazine US)

www.cosmopolitan.com.au
(online branch of *Cosmopolitan* magazine Australia)

www.ejhs.org
(electronic journal of human sexuality)

www.menshealth.co.uk
(online branch of *Men's Health* magazine UK)

www.menshealth.com
(online branch of *Men's Health* magazine US)

www.menshealth.com.au
(online branch of *Men's Health* magazine Australia)

www.menshealthsa.co.za
(online branch of *Men's Health* magazine South Africa)

www.newscientist.com
(online branch of *New Scientist* magazine)

www.ticklekitty.com
(sexpert Sadie Allison's website)

www.wikipedia.org
(online encyclopedia)

Universities and research centers

McGill University Health Centre in Montreal, Canada

Psychology Department, University of Chicago

Smell and Taste Treatment and Research Foundation, Chicago

Psychology Department, University of California Los Angeles

Index

C

K

L

O

R

S

T

W

Y

About the Author

Siski Green is *Men's Health* magazine's sex and relationships writer. She has won writing awards two years running while working at Natmag-Rodale publishing company—one for best feature writer, and the other for best editorial duo. Her no-nonsense attitude and friendly, approachable tone make Siski's writing extremely popular with readers.